ADHD Treatment Follow-Up Study: May, 2000

Even though, after treating ADHD children and their families for years it was clear that CAER treatment was very effective; it was finally time to do a systematic quantitative follow-up study. The results strongly support my clinical impression that CAER makes dramatic improvements in all aspects of the constellation of symptoms comprising ADHD/ADD, without the use of medications. It should be noted that these are some of the most difficult ADHD children around. Parents don't spend the time and money to fly to Spokane until they have exhausted all closer and cheaper alternatives.

Over the last 2 years (98, 99) I saw 74 children, and their families, who could be clearly diagnosed as ADHD/ADD. Their ages ranged from 6 to 17 years. Seventy six percent were males the balance females. Ninety six percent had previously been treated with psychotropic medications, such as Ritalin, Cylert, Adderall, Dexedrine, Chlonadine, Paxil, etc.

We were able to contact 49 parents by telephone to administer a short questionnaire about the effects of CAER treatment on their ADHD/ADD child. To avoid a short-term placebo or honey-moon-effect, only families 6 months or more post-treatment were contacted. All families were treated with three multi-hour intensive treatment sessions over three days.

Overall results were:
86% rated it as Very Effective
6% rated it as Effective
8% rated it as No Different
None rated it as harmful.

None of the children in the Very Effective or Effective categories had been placed on psychotropic medications. Of the children rated No
86% rated it as Very Effective
6% rated it as Effective

Behavior Change At Home:
81% rated their child's behavior as Much Better
11% rated their child's behavior as Better
8% rated their child's behavior as No Different
None rated it as harmful

Behavior Change At School:
76% rated their child's behavior as Much Better
13% rated their child's behavior as Better
11% rated their child's behavior as No Different
None rated it as harmful

ADHD: A PATH TO SUCCESS

A Revolutionary Theory and New Innovation in Drug-Free Therapy

Lawrence Weathers, Ph.D.

Ponderosa Press, Spokane, Washington

ADHD: A Path to Success

A Revolutionary Theory and New Innovation in Drug-Free Therapy

By Lawrence Weathers, Ph.D.

Published by:
Ponderosa Press
6921 E Jamieson Rd.
Spokane, WA 99223 U.S.A.

Copyright 1998 by Lawrence Weathers
First Printing 1998
Second Printing 2001
Third Printing 2004
Printed in the United States of America

Library of Congress Cataloging-in-Publication Data
Weathers, Lawrence R.
ADHD: A Path to Success: A Revolutionary Theory and New Innovation in Drug-Free Therapy / by Lawrence Weathers
Includes bibliographical references and index.
ISBN 0-9659513-1-6 (soft)
1. Attention Deficit Hyperactivity Disorder
2. Attention Deficit Disorder
3. Psychology
4. Psychotherapy
97-92384 CIP

TABLE OF CONTENTS

Cues: PET Studies · Problems with the Logic of PET Studies · The Misuses of Statistics: Correctional Inference · What About Learned Physiological Differences in Neurochemistry? · The Science · Clinical Experience · ADHD Testing: Descriptive vs. Diagnostic · The Bottom-line on the Clinical Relevance of ADHD Testing · Anxious to Diagnose ADHD ... "We've Got to do Something About This" · Opposition to the Ritalin Mandate

is U-Shaped · Daniel – A 9-Year-Old Behavior Problem ·
Building the Reinforcement Bridge · Why Ritalin Alone
Doesn't Work Long-Term · Windows of Opportunity · Missing
the Window of Opportunity

Acknowledgments

This is the book that never could have been it were not for the help of many other people. First, the most important person, **Mary B. Weathers, Ph.D.**, wife, psychologist, photographer and business partner. As a wife, she put up with my long hours of rambling discussions as I talked over kid after kid, idea after idea. As my fellow psychologist and professional compatriot she plowed through rough early versions making insightful corrections and providing encouragement all the way. She polished the final draft to perfection. As a photographer she took the pictures for the cover. As my business partner, she has been the glue that kept our practice together while I have been preoccupied with writing this book. She is also the co-author of our soon to be released book, *Couples: A Path to Success.*

Suzy Spencer hammered my academic sound words into smooth flowing prose. She added the "ands and buts" at the beginning of sentences because she said it made an easier read. She gave me the first outside professional feedback that the ADHD kid had finally passed English 101. Suzy Spencer has been a working writer for more than 20 years with non-fiction articles published in FORTUNE, PEOPLE, MODERN MATURITY, and Los Angeles magazines and short fiction pieces published in the LOS ANGELES HERALD-EXAMINER. She has also contributed to two books. She earned a Masters of Professional Writing degree in fiction from the University of Southern California and a Masters of Business Administration in finance and marketing also from U.S.C.

She is the recipient of two Chilton Editorial Awards, the Austin Writers' League, Word is Art Award, and is a three-time semi-finalist in the Pirates' Alley, Faulkner Awards. She is currently completing her first true crime novel. *Burning Desires*, to be published by Pinnacle Books in 1998.

Kelsey Loughlin took my rough, stick man cartoon ideas and turned them into the lovable and communicative cartoon characters you find in these pages. Her background includes an eclectic mix of mechanical engineering, watercolor cartooning, and mountain climbing. The majority of her cartooning involves commissioned work, with images of comically distressed mountain climbers in hopeless predicaments—images inspired by 10 years spent exploring mountains of the world.

Virginia Bott, Ph.D. waded through my early draft, reorganizing and hammering my prose. She is a Professor of Political Science at California State University. Her publications include a book entitled *Blacks and Bureaucracy* as well as, numerous articles related to street-level bureaucracy, public personnel administration, and city manager government.

Pricilla DeWolf shouldered the job of pouring over an early draft to refine my prose a step further. She is the mother of four.

Jill Espy, my office manager, compulsively attended to the endless details of moving a book from words, to a tool for parents of ADHD children. Without her, this manuscript would still be a file on my hard drive.

Dirk Tuell is the artist who created the front, spine, and back cover. He also typeset the book. More of his work can be seen at *http://www.livinggraphics.com*

Warning-Disclaimer

When you write a book it is stylistically very difficult to put in every cautionary, qualifying, provisional statement that might be appropriate. So let me clarify the intention and limitations of this book. This book is intended to provide information on ADHD. It is sold with the understanding that neither the publisher nor the author are engaged in rendering parenting, medical or legal advice via this book. If you wish such expert services, you should contract with a competent professional.

This is the story of one psychologist's voyage through his own ADHD, years of working with ADHD patients, as well as the development of a unique theory and treatment technology. It is my story, what I believe in and what I have done with my patients. This book is not meant to represent that I have the answer to any specific child's problems. I can only tell you what I have learned. You must decide the relevance of my story to your child and family.

Every effort has been made to make the information in this book as complete and accurate as possible. However, I am not perfect, nor is my book. There may be mistakes both typographical and in the content. Therefore this book should be used as a general guide and not as the ultimate source for your decisions about treatment.

The purpose of this book is to educate and entertain. The author and Ponderosa Press shall have neither liability nor responsibility to any person or entity with respect to any loss or damage caused, or alleged to be caused, directly or indirectly by the information contained in this book.

If you do not wish to be bound by the above, you may return this book to the publisher for a full refund.

Introduction

Life Through the Eyes of an Attention Deficit Hyperactivity Disorder Child

With terror in my heart, I can still remember sitting in emotional and almost physical pain at Palm Elementary School in Beaumont, California. It was fourth grade, and what was going on in the classroom was beyond my attention. That's because my mind had escaped. Looking out the window was my only escape from the endless monotony of the classroom.

Being "jerked back" when the teacher called on me, was overwhelming and nauseating. I felt I had missed so much while being "spaced out" that the demands seemed insurmountable. I had no clue where to begin.

Since I felt little hope of being rewarded for my feeble efforts, my biggest desire was to escape on another mental vacation. That is exactly what I did. My mind traveled out the window again — even though I dimly knew that I was digging myself into a deeper hole. As self-defeating as this strategy was, it was my only defense.

My understanding of Attention Deficit Hyperactivity Disorder is deeply rooted in my own experience. I was an ADHD child. I am now a Ph.D. Clinical Psychologist with a thriving and successful practice.

Parents, there is hope for you and your ADHD child.

Why My Interest in ADHD

Professionally, I have been working with ADHD children since 1971. For the first twenty years I read the books, took courses, and did the therapy as prescribed. As hard as I tried to make it work, the theoretical picture did not seem to fit the children I was seeing, nor did the prescribed therapy approaches prove very useful.

In 1991, I began to develop a radically different approach to psychotherapy for all of my patients, ADHD and others. This led to the invention of a computerized psychotherapy machine, Computer Aided Emotional Restructuring (CAER).

Computer Aided Emotional Restructuring is a new, patented, treatment that sprang from another new therapy, Eye Movement Desensitization and Reprocessing (EMD/R). (EMD/R is fully explained in chapter 24).

Unlike traditional therapies, CAER does not depend much on talking. Rather, it taps powerful neurological mechanisms to elicit deep relaxation and vivid mental imagery. When these two effects are juxtaposed, pathology-producing emotions are extinguished through a process called desensitization.

More simply put, CAER uses lights and sound to help the ADHD child enter a relaxed state. Then, the relaxed and calm child, with the aid and supervision of a therapist, imagines an anxiety-provoking situation — such as school. Quickly, the relaxed state erases the anxiety state so that school, or whatever the provoker might be, no longer causes stress in the child.

No drugs are used at all.

Initially I used Computer Aided Emotional Restructuring on my adult patients who had a variety of common problems such as depression, anxiety, phobias and marriage problems. The results were exciting. Many times these problems were eradicated in just a few sessions.

Therefore, I began to extend the procedure to other problems not commonly addressed by EMD/R, including ADHD. Even with my early, primitive CAER machines, the results were striking.

I really did not know why CAER works, but two different sources began to yield insights. By reflecting on my own difficult school history and listening to the ADHD children themselves, my understanding developed. These children were telling me about feelings and experiences that I could remember well from my own school years.

That's why ADHD: A Path to Success is a story of hope for parents of ADHD children. It is a personal story. It is my story. It is the success story of my patients.

Chapter 1

ADHD – Adaptive, Not Defective

Chris, a Six-Year-Old Boy with Attention Deficit Hyperactivity Disorder

C hris* was a cute, freckle-faced, six-year-old boy who embodied my image of Tom Sawyer. Only in the first grade, Chris was already falling behind in his schoolwork. His teacher described him as constantly disrupting the class by speaking out of turn, touching other children, being out of his seat, and playing with toys rather than doing his work.

Occasionally Chris would get into fistfights with other children. He did not start such conflicts, but when provoked, Chris spared no effort or tactic to win. And he always did win.

Chris' mother brought this young "Tom Sawyer" to me for an evaluation for Attention Deficit Hyperactivity Disorder (ADHD). This was at the school's insistence. The teacher was resolute in her belief that Chris had ADHD and must be put on stimulant medication.

* All names have been changed in order to maintain the individual's privacy.

Since Chris' mother strongly objected to this recommendation, she instead brought Chris to me, a psychologist with a new, drug-free, alternative treatment.

After only three sessions using Computer Aided Emotional Restructuring (CAER), Chris' behavior at school and home improved markedly. Yet at age six, Chris was at the lower limit developmentally to benefit from CAER.

Three years after his initial visit, follow-up evaluations have revealed no further academic or behavior problems. Chris is still doing well at home and school.

If you know anything about traditional psycho-therapy or theories of ADHD, the best thing you can do is forget it for now. Goethe said it well: "It is impossible to learn something you think you already know." So for now, getting dumb is the most brilliant thing you can do.

Computer Aided Emotional Restructuring is a treatment technology that extinguishes ineffective emotional patterns quickly, effectively, and without drugs.

As the title implies, "emotional restructuring" demands cooperation from the patient in order to dredge up unpleasant memories. These unpleasant memories are often the root of physiological and psychological problems.

With Chris, I asked him to think about people who made him mad. This included his teacher, some of his fellow students at school, some boys at day care who would not let him play, and his big brother. Chris liked doing this. He said it made him "think about things."

At the end of session one, which included an initial evaluation and beginning treatment using CAER, Chris' mother was given a five-minute cassette tape and instruction sheet to take to the teacher.

The teacher was asked to record her "behavioral control instructions" such as "Put that in your desk," "Keep your hands to yourself," and "Sit on your bottom."

During sessions two and three using CAER, this same tape was played. Once again, Chris was asked to think about people who made him angry. He reported that this tape made him mad. He also said that after he had listened to the tape a few times, it did not make him angry.

By the end of the third session, Chris did not seem to have any emotional response to the tape. The powerful feelings that were at the root of Chris' behavioral problems were extinguished by CAER.

I also saw Chris' mother for one session. This was to alleviate her own guilt about putting firm limits on her son. Abused and rejected in her own childhood, she was overreacting in her determination to avoid the same patterns with Chris.

Although she had an excellent command of behavior management concepts, she could not effectively put them into practice because doing so made her feel terrible. In fact, whenever she tried to be firm with Chris, his complaining made her feel like the "Wicked Witch of the West."

After one session using CAER to re-experience her own unsettling emotions, Chris' mother was able to do an excellent job of systematically rewarding and punishing Chris. That's because such actions no longer tapped into her own emotional history.

With the help of CAER, ADHD can be overcome.

ADHD Demographics

ADHD is a major problem occurring in as many as 3.5 million children in the United States, or three to seven percent of the nation's children, according to various estimates. No one really knows the exact number. The male-to-female ratio is about two to one.

Its common characteristics are:

1)   Fidgeting with the hands or feet

2)   Difficulty remaining seated

3)   Difficulty awaiting taking turns in games

4)   Difficulty following through on instructions

5)   Shifting from one uncompleted task to another

6)   Difficulty playing quietly

7)   Interrupting conversations and intruding into other children's games

8)   Appearing to not be listening to what is being said

9)   Doing things that are dangerous without thinking about the consequences

Currently ADHD is thought of as a neurological disorder that affects motivational systems. Accepted treatment consists of behavior therapy and/or stimulant drugs.

These treatments are usually helpful, but the child's behavior seldom becomes normal. When either of these treatments is withdrawn, behavior most often regresses.

That's because the treatments only manage and do not cure the pathology (Barkley, 1990).

Myths of ADHD

Traditional thoughts about ADHD impose a number of damaging myths onto children like Ryan. These myths have led to many ineffective approaches for treating ADHD.

Let's compare traditional views of ADHD with my view of children like Ryan.

Traditional View	**My View**
ADHD Children are defective and disabled.	ADHD is a very refined adaptive skill.
There may be neurological problems in ADHD children.	Neurological problems are irrelevant because ADHD is learned.
An ADHD Child's mental processes are strange, unusual or defective.	ADHD children think just like we do.
Ritalin improves children's performance.	Ritalin helps parents and teachers, not children.

When people describe a specific ADHD child, I'm often left with an image of the kid with a clock mainspring spiraling out of his head and gears raining down. If all of his gears and springs were in right, if his broken parts were fixed, he would work and do what we want.

ADHD children are not clocks with a broken mainspring and gears falling out.

In fact, we do treat the child as if he were a broken mechanical device like a watch. But we use professional words such as "disorder."

We do this because a medical diagnosis denoting disorder, brokenness, or deviancy makes ADHD more socially acceptable. As neat and circumscribed as this approach seems, it does not capture the diffuse, culturally enmeshed nature of the problem.

In truth, the ADHD child does not have a "disorder." He is not broken.

He has just learned adaptive strategies that we do not like. He resorts to ADHD behavior, not because his gears and springs are not meshing, but because it works, and it works well. The gears of an ADHD child mesh with perfect precision, expertly propelling him away from his discomforts.

We, as parents and teachers, just happen to find his strategy in conflict with our own agendas. Simply put, we think if you are not like me or do not do what I want, you are deviant or disordered. Thus, I am order; you, disorder. This is incorrect thinking.

The ADHD child is a highly trained and skilled adapter to a painful situation. The mechanisms that he uses are exactly the ones the rest of us use on a daily basis. However, within the closed, repetitive conditioning situation of schools, these adaptive strategies are exaggerated and ultimately backfire.

Chapter 2

ADHD: Historical Change in Labeling the Disorder

Luke, a 14-Year-Old ADHD Boy

Luke was a recalcitrant bully who had struggled with both behavior and learning problems since his earliest school days. In fact, his academic performance was in the barely passing range.

When Luke hit third grade, he was referred to a pediatrician, who diagnosed him as ADHD and began treating Luke with Ritalin. The effect of the stimulant was immediately positive, and Luke's parents thought the problem was solved.

But in less than a year, his behavior and grades again began to decline. Over the next several years, his parents and doctor tried a variety of behavioral approaches. At the same time, they were periodically putting him on and taking him off his stimulant medications. Nothing seemed to work and the family frustration level rose.

By the time the family arrived in my office, Luke had been thrown out of two schools and was temporarily expelled from his current school. His records indicated that he had at one time or other carried diagnosis of ADHD, BD, and LD. He was covering his embarrassment about his poor academic showing by fighting with his classmates. He took pride in the fear he provoked in his peers.

He also turned his intimidation skills on his mother, who was particularly vulnerable to his tactics because of her chronic and occasionally severe depression.

I had Luke make emotionally provocative audio tapes for each of his parents, and they jointly made one for him. Luke then spent seven sessions on CAER reviewing the tape his parents had made as well as his anxious, frustrating, angry and demeaning academic experiences.

He remembered the times he was laughed at in class, when teachers were mad at him, when he felt like a failure, as well as when his peers made him angry and hurt his feelings. As these feelings abated, his behavior at home and school improved.

At this point, though both parents were involved in Luke's therapy, the focus turned to mother and son and dealing with the emotional history that caused Luke's mother's depression and Luke's academic anxiety and anger.

Luke's mother spent six CAER sessions reviewing her background of neglect and abuse, which laid beneath her depression. As her depression lifted, she became better able to administer systematic discipline for Luke's antics without caving in or feeling guilty. To her surprise, as she became firmer and more consistent with Luke, he respected her more, wanted to spend more time with her, and became more compliant.

Luke's father spent three sessions extinguishing the resentments toward his wife that kept him from being a fully cooperative parent, as well as the resentment that he had built up toward Luke for all the years of family uproar he had caused. These emotional changes led him to be a more supportive husband and a more engaged father.

After Luke, his mother, and his father had all taken their turns in the CAER machine, extinguishing their responses to the tapes, the family conflict was minimal, and

Luke now gets B's and C's with little effort. He is no longer a bully at home or school.

Three-year follow-up indicates that these changes are stable. Luke is now in his senior year of high school. He plans to attend the community college next year. His mother has had no reoccurrence of depression. His mom and dad are finding more things to share and spend more time together.

ADHD, Current State of the Art Debunked

Numerous names have been given to the learning and behavioral problems that are common in children today. These labels represent non-distinct, overlapping categories that are often used as much on the basis of current popularity or the availability of funding as on the characteristics of the child.

Because of this, many children carry multiple labels, either at the same time or across time. The three most common labels used today are Attention Deficit Hyperactivity Disorder (ADHD), Learning Disabilities, and Behavior Disabilities.

Since categorization and diagnostic efforts have primarily focused on describing and measuring the alleged differences between these types of children's problems, there has been little interest in understanding the predominant commonalties they share. Yet, they are simply variations of the same theme, and they are far more alike than different.

Therefore, my efforts have been directed toward understanding the common forces that drive children who carry any of these three diagnoses and finding effective treatment for the shared patterns — contrary to the interests of most investigators in this area. And since ADHD is the most inclusive of the three disorders, the following discussion begins with it and then shows the relationship to Learning Disabilities and Behavior Disabilities.

History of ADHD Labeling and Treatment

Over the years, numerous labels have been given to children with ADHD. In the 1960s they were called brats. With the growing medicalization of common problems, they were labeled Minimal Brain Dysfunction. As behaviorism became popular, they were called hyperactive. Eventually these children were labeled Attention Deficit Disorder, or ADD.

From the last two labels evolved the currently accepted diagnosis of Attention Deficit Hyperactivity Disorder, ADHD. There seemed to be something curative about finding exactly the right name for these troubled children.

ADHD was originally thought of as a neurological disorder that damaged a child's ability to focus his attention. During the 1970s, stimuli of the outside world were seen as involuntarily intruding into the patient's consciousness, similar to how delusions intrude into a schizophrenic's consciousness.

These children were thought to be unable to filter out unwanted intrusions. Their attention was dragged to and fro by whatever surrounded them. In other words, children were helpless victims of environmental stimuli.

Treatment during this era consisted in part of placing the child into a low-distraction environment — such as a quiet study booth with nothing on the walls. Classrooms with high or few windows were built. The idea was to reduce the number of potential distractions that might lure the child from the desired task.

This approach went through its placebo-effect period of success. With increasing experience, however, the placebo effect wore off, and windowless rooms did not seem to be of much help. In moments of desperation, though, this treatment is still occasionally used.

Treatment efforts were then directed toward teaching children to "control themselves," meaning control their own attention levels. The idea was that the children lacked the skills to control their own wandering minds.

Since this was a nice philosophical fit with the educational setting in which most of the children were identified and treated, an action plan was easily developed. Children were taught cognitive behavior therapy techniques.

This means they were taught to think differently about problems and to talk to themselves in special ways, ways that would help them make "better choices" — as if the children had chosen to be ADHD in the first place.

In a recent consultation with school staffers of an ADHD child I was treating, I was struck by what the principal said.   She proudly explained in detail that whenever Brandon, the ADHD child in question, misbehaved, she would take him into her office and "go over what choices he had and each of their consequences."

What Brandon really got was the undivided attention of the highest status person in the school, in the highest status room in the school.

The principal, counselor, and teacher attending this meeting were so entrenched in their educational/cognitive model that they were completely unaware of the powerful social reinforcement they were providing Brandon for his rather minor acting out behavior.

Bewildered, they could not see why such a rational, logical approach was not working. They could not see the obvious because it lay outside their favored cognitive model.

Cognitive behavior therapy or this "teach the child to think differently" therapy, is still quite prevalent in school-based treatment efforts because it fits philosophically with school administrators, counselors and teachers. Today, teachers still ask children "Why did you do it?" referring to "bad choices," and want the ADHD students to "learn new skills."

Research on cognitive strategies do show some short-term benefits, but the gains fade quickly.

More recently, the notion of distractions intruding on the ADHD child's consciousness is no longer postulated.

ADHD is viewed, instead, as a motivational disorder characterized by quick boredom with rewards (Barkley, 1991). In other words, the child is so easily bored with his reinforcers that he has difficulty focusing his attention on the current activity. This boredom causes the child to search his world for alternative, novel, reinforcing stimuli.

From the child's perspective, seeking alternative stimulus is viewed as an active, adaptive strategy, despite the fact that it is often in conflict with his environment. For our purposes, viewing the child as an active agent versus a passive victim is critical to our understanding. Nintendo's Mario points up the fallacy of the theory that the strength of reinforcers fades. More on that later.

Chapter 3

A Personal Experience of ADHD

Understanding ADHD Thought Process

In order to better understand ADHD, it is imperative to see the ways in which our common, daily experiences are similar to the thinking, feeling, and behavior of an ADHD child. This is important for two reasons.

First, regardless of whether you are a teacher, parent, or researcher, little can be gained until you begin to see the world through the eyes of an ADHD child. Invaluable insights are acquired by mapping the experience of a child through our own personal experience. Formal research experiments can only validate, not originate, these insights.

Secondly, by personalizing the experiences of the ADHD child, we make an important discovery. This discovery flies in the face of traditional medicine, which wants to identify something as broken and fix it, i.e., medicate it.

This discovery, which supports one of my major tenets, is inescapable. This discovery is that ADHD children think the same way we do. Their situation has just trained them to emphasize certain thought patterns more than others. And we use exactly those same thought patterns on a regular basis, just not as often as the ADHD child. In fact, most of us would resort to the same strategies if we were put in the same situation as the ADHD child.

But because we think of ADHD children as being different, because we think they have a "disability," we refuse to give ourselves the same disability label — despite the exact same thinking style.

Yet, ADHD children think no differently than we do.

We Think Like ADHD Children All the Time

Let me illustrate by citing a personal experience. While engaged in the relentless drudgery of writing the computer program logic and voice prompts for CAER, I was having trouble concentrating. My attention constantly drifted off after I wrote each sentence. I continually caught myself looking out the window, going to the bathroom, making a telephone call, or looking at a magazine.

With great effort, I brought myself back to the tedious, repetitive task at hand — writing another sentence. A large cup of espresso coffee helped increase my willful control over my attention. With the coffee, I temporarily regained the power to make my mind do the required task for a little longer.

Finally, after hours of this struggle, I logged onto the Internet. In just a few seconds, my attention and energy improved dramatically, though I had not changed my position at the very same computer, the very same desk, next to the very same window.

My attention went unbroken for the next hour as I searched the Internet for things that interested me.

Thinking back over this scenario, I see my experience exactly parallels that of the ADHD child. I was forcing myself to do a dreaded task, much as a teacher forces a child to do his work in the classroom.

My writing the computer system was very similar to the ADHD child doing math or spelling. Both of our tasks required continuous, sequential attention to detail. Both were repetitive of a similar process with detailed variations. Both were boring because of the repetition, and both of us were required to do the task to achieve a goal.

Though I could keep my body at the task just as the teacher keeps the child at his desk, the unpleasantness of both our tasks soon conditioned our attention to switch to more interesting things. For the child it might be staring out the window, playing with an eraser, talking to a friend in the next row, or wandering around the classroom. For me, it was staring out the window, making a phone call, and reading a magazine.

We both achieved relief from these boring tasks by automatically, against my conscious intention or the teacher's will, learning to avoid the aversive tasks by shifting our attention away from them — "spacing out" or becoming distracted. Relative to the tasks assigned to us, we each had an "attention" deficit and were being "hyperactive."

In fact, my cup of espresso worked just like the child's dose of Ritalin (or Dexedrine or Cylert). Ritalin allows the child to focus his attention on his work in order to please his teacher. Caffeine helps me to force my mind to do what I want it to do, as opposed to helplessly following my learned defense patterns and not performing a tedious task that I don't want to do.

Both Ritalin and caffeine help us redirect our attention back to the task we intentionally wish to address. Both Ritalin and caffeine are powerful central nervous system stimulants.

(As a sidelight, before stimulant drugs came into widespread use, mothers of ADHD children discovered that a cup or two of coffee in the morning would help their youngsters survive the morning hours in school.)

My time on the Internet also worked like a child's time on Nintendo. As many parents know, ADHD children can attend to Nintendo for hours, even though they may have been very distracted from the school work that immediately preceded it. My ability to focus my attention rebounded in exactly the same way when I logged on to the Internet.

The Internet and Nintendo share a common feature in that they have no negative history that make a person want to "space out" instead of doing the needed work. At our chosen tasks our attention was flawless. It would seem to take a very peculiar neurological deficit to account for such sudden variation in both of our attentional patterns.

Do I have ADHD? I doubt it as much as I doubt that most kids labeled as such have ADHD, at least as it is normally conceptualized as a neurological disorder. We have to give up the idea that the ADHD child's mental processes are strange, unusual, defective or inferior. They are just one more variation of the perceptual distortion that all of us use everyday to survive in an often-crazy world.

Your Personal Experience of ADHD

One way Zen masters teach meditation is through painting. But before a Zen master will let you paint a flower, he insists that you become the flower.

You must meditate on it until you no longer just see it. You must experience it and know it as part of you. Only after you understand the flower in that depth, does the Zen master believe can you meaningfully paint the flower.

This is even truer when you are trying to "paint" the transient nature of attention. Not only is cognitive understanding not enough, it is, in fact, not even useful.

Let us try an experiment that will help us move beyond a mere intellectual understanding of the distractibility of an ADHD child. Stop reading now and think back over your own experience of having to do some boring, repetitive task for a very long time.

Remember how easy it was to space out or become distracted.

Did you ever try some coffee to help get you back on task? How did it work?

Remember how easy it was to focus your attention on other tasks that captured your interest.

Compare your attention under these two conditions — boring task vs. interesting task. If you can do this, you have walked in the ADHD child's shoes, and you have taken a major step in helping them.

Personal History of ADHD

My formal learning career started off poorly. I am told I never stopped moving. I took everything apart — a toy, a clock, or the house.

Though my teachers seemed to like me, I was always in conflict with my peers. I was a big kid, and my clumsiness put me on the short end of such fights.

My issues were not confined to school, like most kids with school and learning difficulties. I had more important things on my mind -- my parents' fighting. Thinking about their battles made it hard for me to focus on school.

Even though their fights were limited to strong words, their hostilities preoccupied my mind. My emotional arousal was too high for any real learning to take place. I was worried and anxious. These conflicts with students and parents took precedence over school. Soon I fell behind my peers.

This started a destructive chain of events. I began to get negative feedback from students and teachers. This in turn made me feel anxious when I had to answer in class or was put in any evaluative situation.

My repeated failure at academic tasks, particularly reading, sparked raw terror in me. In elementary school, we had regular reading circles. Six or eight kids would sit around in a circle taking turns reading.

I would sit there in a cold sweat as my turn came closer and closer. It was my teacher's version of Edgar Allen Poe's "The Pit and the Pendulum." The reading blade kept coming closer and closer.

To try to save face, I would count the number of children before my turn to read and try to calculate which paragraph I would be expected to read. Then I would go over and over this paragraph trying to work out every word. I would try to memorize it because I knew I was so anxious that there was no way I could actually read it in front of the other kids and teacher.

Despite and because of my high anxiety efforts, I usually botched even the simplest reading task. I became even more humiliated, embarrassed, angry, depressed, and degraded. I could think of few things in life worse than reading.

What was more sinister than Poe was that the reading blade did not kill you. You would have to face the reading blade the same way tomorrow, and the next day, and the next day for what seemed the rest of your life.

Several times a week a remedial reading teacher would take me and some of the other "dummies" out of the classroom for an hour or so, to practice our reading.

I was always aware of being in the "sparrow" reading group because everyone knew that it was for the dumb kids. (In spite of adult efforts, kids quickly pick up on the real facts.) And yet, I cannot remember any different procedures being used by this teacher than had been used by my regular classroom teacher.

Though her efforts were valiant and well intended, they were just another dose of the same old toxic solution that I eventually learned was the source of my problems. I made little progress.

How could I? To me, reading was associated with school, reading groups, reading out loud, peer ridicule, and poor self-image.

The harder the teacher tried, the more upset I became, the worse I did, the dumber I got. I saw this as just another opportunity to face the terror of the reading blade. I began to fight passively the very process of what felt like stuffing things down my throat. I did not learn to read until I was in the seventh grade.

Eventually, I did learn to read, not because of more sophisticated efforts by my teachers, but because I developed a driving need to know, literally. I was interested in hot rods.

I wanted to know about the most technical aspects of cam timing, fuel injection, and suspension systems.

Since no one in my world, including my car mechanic father, had an in-depth knowledge about these things, the only way to learn about them was to read.

At first, the reading was difficult. I picked through articles word by word, read captions on pictures, and guessed a lot. Despite the difficulty, I was powerfully motivated to decode this information system that held the key to what I wanted to know.

Within two weeks, I was reading well. And reading was no longer the terrifying school subject that made me feel incompetent. In fact, it was part of a world that had nothing to do with school. It was something I did alone at home for hours, pouring over hot rod books and magazines. Alone at home, reading was easy and fun. Alone at home, it became my bridge from one world to another, simply through my urgent need to know about hot rods.

Also on my own, away from school, unbeknownst to my peers, parents or teachers, I had worked out my own simple system of trigonometry. My methods even included basic look-up tables for a variety of what I later realized were standard trig functions. This was my own private system of calculation not a trigonometry that I had learned in school. Thank goodness I did not even know a discipline of trigonometry existed. If I had made the association with math in school, likely this calculation system would have been stymied by the transfer of negative emotions from school.

Rather than this calculation system coming out of school assignments, it rose out of a curious observation. One night while riding in the back seat of my parent's car-watching search lights bounce off of a low cloud ceiling. I wanted to figure out a way to determine how high the clouds were by measuring the angle of the searchlight and the distance between the searchlight and the spot directly under where the light bounced off the cloud. It was a very practical concern, not a math homework problem that drove my thinking. The first round of calculation was on the fog on the back window of my parent's car. Thank goodness it was a large back window. That happened when I was in the fifth grade.

My newly acquired skills also began to have payoffs outside my bedroom. The formerly dumb kid now had the keys to unlock the rest of the school tasks. Those were the days of Evelyn Woods teaching JFK speed reading, and I became adept at speed-reading. By the end of high school, I had become the fastest reader in the school. This did not mean that all academic hurdles had been solved with one fell swoop, but a giant step had been made. I was easily getting A's and B's, but I still felt like the dumb kid.

I am sure Mr. Hurd, my 8th grade English teacher would have been shocked by my improved grades. In order to take Spanish in high school I had to get permission from Mr. Hurd. When I presented him with the form to sign he took me to a large cloak area in back of the classroom so we could talk privately. I will always remember what he said, "I will sign this because you are a nice kid. But, as soon as it gets too hard, drop it. If you work hard we think you can graduate from high school." Then he signed the form. I was hurt, angry, determined, and confused. A sense of determination welled in me, and stayed with me for years there after. I would show him.

To you, Mr. Hurd, it is "Doctor Weathers."

I only went to college because a high school counselor noticed I was getting good grades and called me into his office. When he suggested that I consider going to college, I had no idea where to find one. I was so naive about education that I was shocked when, during my junior year of high school, the school superintendent got his doctorate and then did not open an office to practice medicine. I didn't know there were any people other than physicians who had the title of doctor.

Despite the gains, despite the fact that I now have my own doctorate degree and am called Dr. Weathers, the scars from the reading circle are still within. To this day, I avoid reading aloud if at all possible. But reading and trig were exciting mental adventures for me. And these isolated contemplations were to me what Nintendo is to the current crop of ADHD kids.

Like Nintendo, my trig and reading about hot rods had no relationship to my failure experiences. There was no negative learning history associated with them. Without the anxiety, I could learn quickly. In a similar way, the treatment proposed in this book, CAER, extinguishes the anxiety, so that formerly ADHD children can learn easily.

Chapter 4

The Conditioned Attentional
Avoidance Loop Model

Developmental Vulnerability to Family Conflict and ADHD

Clinically, ADHD children appear to be exposed to many and sometimes severe early stresses. In fact, in the hundreds of families I have worked with, I have seldom found an ADHD child from a family that did not have a history of problems.

Marital conflict, parental illness, divorce, economic strife, verbal or physical abuse, or one of many other things are often the stressors. Few of these ADHD children seem to come from stable "Leave it to Beaver" families.

This may be one reason why twice as many boys as girls have ADHD. Boys develop more slowly, so more of them would be ill-prepared to cope with such problems. And being forced to deal with such early stresses shapes the child's ability to focus his attention.

In other words, since the child is forced to deal with disturbing stimuli in an unpleasant environment, he develops a preferred, attentional style — he avoids the unpleasant by focusing his attention elsewhere.

This is called attentional avoidance ... the Conditioned Attentional Avoidance Loop.

Conditioned Attentional Avoidance Loop Model

The Conditioned Attentional Avoidance Loop Model hypothesizes that ADHD behavior could be a result of a child's exposure to interpersonal stress before the child is developmentally equipped to handle it.

Indeed, attentional avoidance may be the only mechanism for a young child to escape these early stresses, since their physical mobility to escape is restricted and they do not have the verbal or intellectual skills to change the stressor.

Once this adaptive strategy garners some negative reinforcement, it is refined and resorted to more and more frequently. When the stresses of school arrive, the child has a well-refined escape mechanism to deal with the new demands. It works well for young children and we call it ADHD.

According to the Conditioned Attentional Avoidance Loop Model, ADHD children avoid negative emotional experiences and direct their attention elsewhere via anger, performance anxiety, social deprecation, frustration, and ultimately boredom.

They do this much like a baby turning its head away from something it does not like. Thus, ADHD is not a deficit, defect, or deficiency. It is a highly skilled, coping mechanism that, at the moment, serves the child.

The thought of doing math makes him angry and depressed, feelings he would just as soon avoid. Although he dislikes the feelings he experiences during math class, he cannot physically avoid being in math class every day. He finds that if he fantasizes about skate boarding, being in math class does not feel as bad.

PAIN-FREE MATH CLASS

Over time, due to negative reinforcement, he learns to fantasize sooner, better, and more automatically. He effectively develops greater protection from the feelings he used to get from math class.

Negative reinforcement is an often-misunderstood concept. Unlike common usage, it is not equivalent to punishment. It is like lying on the beach in the sun until you are very hot and uncomfortable, then terminating this aversive overheating, by getting in the cold water. This temperature change is experienced as positive change. This positive feeling of cooling off thereby reinforces dunking in the water when you have become too hot.

Therefore, negative reinforcement is the cessation of aversive stimuli, which by contrast to the aversion, is experienced as a positive or reinforcing change.

There are at least two other positive feedback loops that further exacerbate this process of learned attentional avoidance.

First, the refinement of attentional avoidance further reduces a child's awareness of, and participation in, schoolwork. The child eventually begins to slip involuntarily into conditioned attentional avoidance and, as a result, he spends more and more time in his "own little world."

Second, the teacher is shaped into being more demanding and coercive through negative reinforcement because of the short-term positive benefit of such efforts. This short-term success shapes increasing long-term negativeness in the teacher.

The first process works like this:

As the teacher becomes more determined and insistent that the child do his work "or else," the experience of being in school becomes more negative to the child. So any mental escape he manages (and he will escape many times) is even more negatively reinforcing than it had been previously. That's because it affords successful escape from an increasingly noxious situation.

Second, this negative reinforcement teaches faster and stronger attentional avoidance so that, next time, the teacher must be even more demanding to get the same result.

The escalation of the teacher trying to control the child and the decreasing functioning of the ADHD child is a regularly observed pattern in school settings. Yet, the cause and effect relationship between these two sets of behaviors is not generally understood.

In summary, the ADHD child's decreasing performance elicits more negative feedback from the teacher. The more negative feedback used by the teacher to exact (temporary) compliance and improved performance, the more negative reinforcement the child has for learning more effective attentional avoidance skills. The child is then in a downward spiral that feeds on itself.

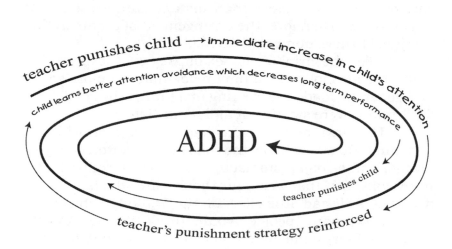

There is also a more general and damaging level of conditioning going on with the ADHD child.

With practice, the child learns to detect, earlier and earlier, links in the chain of events that typically lead to the aversive situation, such as a math assignment.

By sensing and reading the cues earlier and earlier — in fact, even before the original problem shows itself — the escape trigger is pulled sooner and an increasing portion of the child's world is subject to involuntary, conditioned attentional avoidance. He automatically "checks out" in a wider variety of situations as time goes on.

Continuing the above example, the child now learns to avoid not only math but also the math book, math homework sheets, the math teacher who gives him these materials, and the math classroom.

Bottom line — his avoidance coping mechanism is being triggered by a multitude of stimuli, which makes him mentally absent more often, in fact, most of the time, which, in turn, makes his performance deteriorate further.

Children's Limited View of Time

For all of us, immediate rewards and punishments rule our behaviors more than distant gratifications and retributions. Therefore, the arrangement of events in time is critical to development of ADHD.

Take the drinker, for example. At the party last night, the alcohol relaxed him, made him feel more social, and generally made the evening more fun. The reinforcers for drinking were significant and immediate.

The next morning, he had a hangover with dry cottonmouth, a headache, the sensation of cotton candy for brains, and a roiling stomach. The next morning, he felt miserable. But that was many hours after the behavior of drinking, so it had little effect on the drinking behavior.

How many people would drink if they got the hangover first, immediately after drinking, and the next morning they felt great? Not many. Next morning's good feelings would be so remote that they would be unlikely to reinforce drinking. But the close proximity of drinking and the hangover would likely suppress drinking.

When the temporal sequence of the same reinforcers and punishers is changed, the effect on the behavior they follow also changes. For young children, this effect is exaggerated, which makes them particularly vulnerable to certain contingencies.

Young children view time quite differently than adults. At the developmental stage between the ages of five and nine, when children are most often developing ADHD, the idea of long-term consequences has little meaning to them. Next week is as far away as next year. Managing the aversiveness of experience here and now is all that matters. Thus, the fact that their attentional avoidance strategies are eventually going to be very costly to them is meaningless.

Attentional patterns leading to ADHD are likely to begin to form long before adults in the child's world begin to notice them. Once the child discovers attentional escape and negative reinforcement they tend to continue.

These attentionally avoidant patterns work when they are first learned and continue to work long after they should have been replaced with more effective strategies. It is difficult for the child to give up something that has worked so well for so long.

At this developmental stage, children are very responsive to short-term rewards and thereby more vulnerable to problems like ADHD that are shaped by an emphasis on short-term contingencies. They are not developmentally ready to use the thinking patterns, i.e., choices that we attempt to impose on them.

Avoidance Conditioning: The Horse Grows Bigger

Avoidance conditioning in children is similar to adult phobic behavior. For example, consider the behavior of the patient who has a horse phobia. The more successful he is at avoiding horses, the more he feels compelled to avoid them.

For the phobic person, being thrown off a horse may have started out as only mildly anxiety producing. As the actual experience gets more remote because of successful avoidance of horses, the memory of being thrown off the horse gets progressively worse. The recall experience elicits more and more fear than the original experience did.

This increased aversiveness of the memory of being around horses makes it more reinforcing to successfully avoid horses, which in turn makes being around horses more fearful, and so on so that a vicious circle develops.

The exact same process unfolds with the regard to the ADHD child.

What was initially a mildly aversive school situation becomes successively more disturbing after many opportunities for successful avoidance. The ADHD child may have started out mildly frustrated or anxious in math class, but after successfully spacing out in class for a while, the remembered experience of math class may be worse than the previously experienced reality of it. It is like being thrown off a horse.

Folk wisdom tells us to climb immediately back on the horse before fear has a chance to grow. And that folk wisdom is very accurate.

Computer Aided Emotional Restructuring provides an efficient psychological tool to climb back on the math horse. At first, the CAER ride on the math horse is emotionally evocative, just like climbing back on a real horse might be. Children often express anger, fear, anxiety, and depression as they mentally re-experience their academic phobias.

But CAER makes it much easier to stay in the saddle until the emotional bucking stops and the scary math beast is tamed and finally becomes emotionally flat.

Chapter 5

ADHD: A Defense Mechanism

Bob, a 14-Year-Old ADHD Boy

Bob, a 14-year-old, was treated for ADHD in three sessions, totaling five hours. Two two-hour sessions were provided because the family lived in a distant rural town.

During Bob's first 30-minute session using CAER, he focused on all the situations that precipitated a "funny feeling in his stomach." He believed this feeling occurred just before he began to lose attention and started disrupting the class. He worked diligently on this subjective experience and systematically extinguished it.

The father, who brought Bob to the therapy sessions, was just as diligent and cooperative. He was given two five-minute cassette tapes. One was for his wife and him to record statements that provoked Bob, the other was for Bob's teacher to do likewise.

Because of bad weather and the long distance, the second session was three weeks after the first, but it was two hours long. At that time, Bob and his father already reported significant changes at home and school.

During that second session, Bob listened repeatedly to the two tapes his parents and teacher had recorded. His initial response to each tape was anger and agitation. This faded to boredom after a few repetitions.

I also used part of the second session to put the father on CAER to extinguish his emotional responses to Bob's provocative behavior.

By the third session there were few behavioral problems left to work on. Bob's behavior was dramatically better, his grades had improved sharply, and his mood was more positive. So in that session, Bob focused on his performance anxiety in academic work and social situations.

ADHD as a Defense Mechanism

The Conditioned Attentional Avoidance Loop Model appears to be radically different, but in actuality it is a logical extension of traditional theories of psychopathology.

Traditional theories, despite their differences, embrace Sigmund Freud's notion that psychopathology is the result of an earlier emotional trauma. The adaptation to that trauma results in the psychopathology.

ADHD works by the same processes and serves the same function as traditional psychological defense mechanisms. In fact, it is best thought of as a defense mechanism favored by children.

Freud talked about how repression, suppression, or denial, are ways of keeping noxious thoughts and memories out of one's consciousness. That is, they are attentional avoidance mechanisms that work just like ADHD.

Freud saw defenses as the patient's active efforts to adapt, but that ultimately, if overused, backfired. So too, it is with ADHD. Framed in terms of Conditioned Attentional Avoidance Loop Model, the patient is as an active, skilled adapter to the environmental stimuli, just as Freud saw his patients. However, in both cases, defense mechanisms have gone awry.

Like all defense mechanisms, avoidance behavior functions as a way to spare the ADHD child the unpleasant emotions — whether they are triggered by internal or external experiences. It does this by keeping annoyances out of consciousness. But the defense strategy suggested by the Conditioned Attentional Avoidance Loop Model is more obvious than traditional defenses since:

1) The behavior of children is less sophisticated and thus more obvious.

2) The noxious stimuli (parents, teachers, and schoolwork) are usually here and now a opposed to in the past or far away.

3) Adults are actively engaged in keeping the child from physically escaping.

4) Much to the chagrin of the observing or diagnosing adult, the defense mechanisms of the ADHD child are often a reaction to the adult.

ADHD is Felt as an Insult by Adults.

This last point deserves further discussion.

My perspective using the Conditioned Attentional Avoidance Loop Model allows me to focus not only on the ADHD child but also on the adults who play an important role in his environment.

Failure to consider the role of adults in the child's world has made it difficult to observe accurately and understand ADHD. That's because the role of the controlling and evaluating adult, whether teacher or parent, is crucial to filling out our picture of the child. The adult is part of the Conditioned Attentional Avoidance Loop and the adult is the one responsible for triggering the attentional avoidance.

The child, simply, is always maneuvering to stay out of reach, and he does this by directing his attention elsewhere. No matter what you ask him, you get evasive, escapist responses — "I don't know," "Doesn't bother me," "Sure, I have lots of friends," or "I don't care."

These responses occur between bouts of looking away, fiddling with things, wandering off mid-conversation, outpouring emotionally, grimacing, or glowering. These responses are an efficient smokescreen that is both difficult and frustrating for the adult to comprehend and respond to rationally.

Seeing the role of the adult as causal to ADHD behavior may at first feel upsetting and disorienting. We do not like to think of ourselves as the target of someone else's defense system. The message received is that the ADHD child is defining you as the enemy whether you like it or not.

This differs from traditional psychology that deals with patients who are defending against some internal or historical experience. The latter is much less aversive than when someone is defending against you. Despite his most caring and benevolent efforts, the ADHD child blots the therapist, parent or teacher out of his or her reality.

In fact, it is the nature of the ADHD child to refuse to connect interpersonally with you or conform to your demands. He does not seem to understand that you are trying to act in his best interests. Instead, suddenly, the adult is on the receiving end of rudeness, rejection, or insults.

Since the adult feels helpless and frustrated in controlling the child's behavior, he or she feels personally affronted. It is as if your well-meant offer of friendship is being rebuffed.

Because of this affront to you and your reality, it's easy to see ADHD children as more defective than they are. Thus, it becomes even more tempting to categorize ADHD children in an unbecoming fashion — as we are likely to do to anyone who rejects us. If the ADHD child does not like us, he must have something wrong with his brain. So we come up with labels like "Minimal Brain Dysfunction" or "neurotransmitter hypothesis," depending on what is in vogue.

While teachers and counselors insist that they are professionals and thereby do not react emotionally to the antics of children, inevitably they do respond. Not to acknowledge this emotional reaction is to blind ourselves to a major piece of the dynamics driving ADHD. We have been seduced into focusing on only one part of the feedback loop— the child.

Jane, a 14-Year-Old ADHD Girl

Jane, a 14-year-old, white female with ADHD, had been adopted at about 18 months. Her life before adoption was largely unknown except that her birth parents were alcohol and drug abusers. Despite this, she exhibited no evidence of Fetal Alcohol Syndrome.

Jane had a long history of treatment beginning in second grade. A wide variety of stimulant medications as well as a Chlonadine patch had been tried unsuccessfully. She also had been taken to numerous psychologists and other professionals to no avail. In spite of the efforts of these professionals, private sector, as well as a special education placement in the public schools, her behavior progressively worsened.

During Jane's first appointment with me, her behavior, although joking and playful, was loud and confrontational. She made her distaste for adults very clear. She wandered around, talked constantly, inter-rupted others, moved objects, and cussed. Her dress and behavior had a strong masculine demeanor.

On a daily basis, her school life was punctuated by open verbal and physical conflict. Being exceptionally strong for her age, she took delight in literally bouncing other boys and girls off the lockers at school. With minimum provocation, she would regularly stand up in class and tell off the school staff with a well-developed vocabulary of expletives.

By the time she was referred to me, Jane was on the verge of being moved from her learning disabilities classes to a behavior disabilities class. Her own words pretty well summed up her situation, "My life is screwed."

Jane was certainly one of the most disturbed ADHD children I have ever seen in practice.

Our first several sessions together were focused on her anger, fear of rejection, and conflicts with peers and teachers. Because of lack of cooperation from the school, we were not able to proceed with desensitization by using tapes made by school staffers.

Her parents, though, were very cooperative, so we were able to do the desensitization tape procedure with them. By the fourth session, her parents reported that Jane showed more affectionate behavior and did homework voluntarily.

Despite the lack of cooperation from the school, by the fifth session Jane's teacher greeted the mother with praise for Jane and how well she was doing in class. At the same time, the teacher suggested that Jane would be able to get out of the Special Ed class and into regular classes if she continued her new performance level.

Jane was not able to move into all regular classrooms because, as the ADHD subsided, her true intellectual limitations became apparent. Despite some very systematic and consistent study efforts on her part, her academic performance, though much improved, was still subnormal. Jane was mildly retarded. She has, however, been successfully mainstreamed into several classes

Though she has a somewhat odd, rambunctious, and endearing social style, it is now within normal limits. She makes friends, participates in activities, and feels good about herself. Over a three year period, Jane was treated in about 35 sessions, most of which were in the first year and a half.

She is now 17 and has not been seen for about 14 months. Follow-up telephone calls indicate that her behavior in school is normal. She is still mostly in special education classes with some mainstreaming. She has occasional minor conflicts with her parents, as is typical of most teenagers. And she is beginning to date successfully.

Chapter 6

Emotional vs. Rational Controls of Behavior

A Learning Model for ADHD: Conditioned Attentional Avoidance Loop Model

If we look at ADHD as learned behavior, and this learning produces measurable physiological changes in the child's brain, these chronic learned patterns are caused by both specific situations and broad cultural influences on the child. ADHD and the associated physiological changes in his brain are the child's adaptation to the world we have put him in, rather than being the result of traditionally hypothesized neurological defects.

The Conditioned Attentional Avoidance Loop Model Makes Neurological Theories Superfluous

There is a long and productive tradition in science to adopt the simplest, most plausible explanation for the observed data. This tradition has been called Occam's Razor. The idea of this philosophical razor is to shave off everything that does not help explain observations. The beauty of this strategy is that it yields the simplest, most elegant explanation of one's observations.

In the case of ADHD, using Occam's Razor to shave off neurological hypotheses from Conditioned Attentional Avoidance Loop Model results in no loss of explanatory power. Conditioned Attentional Avoidance Loop Model is certainly a simpler, more parsimonious explanation of ADHD than neurologically based explanations.

The dictate of Occam's Razor is that once you have the simplest, most effective explanation for a phenomenon, you only further muddle the picture by adding logical curlicues. There is no reason to elaborate the relatively simple explanation of ADHD offered by Conditioned Attentional Avoidance Loop Model with neurological curlicues.

Conditioned Attentional Avoidance Loop Model does not rule out the claim that there is a neurological component. Such a hypothesis just does not add anything. Clinically, it is also more useful to have a theory that emphasizes variables that you can effect. Learned patterns can be changed; defective neurons can not.

First Get Run Over Emotionally, Then Learn to Run, Attentionally

Once the ADHD child is aroused by feelings of anxiety and anger, his ability to learn attentional avoidance increases while his ability to learn math, spelling and the like declines. This happens in a two-stage process.

First, the child experiences both the discomfort of the emotion as well as its negative effects on his performance. And he is overwhelmed by this experience.

Second, he learns to escape this noxious experience through attentional avoidance. Although avoidance feels better in the short run, performance at home and school soon deteriorates.

Fragile Thoughts, Powerful Emotions

The heat of such emotion easily disrupts the calm, cool, and fragile mechanism of human rationality. In fact, emotional responses are much quicker and forceful than logical responses. Emotional responses are instantaneous, whereas a logical consideration of data, options, and a decision will take at minimum a few seconds and may take years.

If the emotional response happens first, the rational response won't materialize. If the rational chain of thoughts is already in progress, it will be preempted by the mobilization of emotion.

That's why the experience of "blanking out" in an emotionally laden situation, particularly, angry confrontations, is common. In the heat of battle we're suddenly inarticulate. Later, after emotions have cooled, we have greater access to our intellectual abilities. All the things we wish we had said become obvious.

In the heat of battle, did we develop a neurological abnormality, ADHD, or a learning disability? No! No more than the ADHD child does in the classroom. Rather, our emotional arousal temporarily supplanted our intellectual process. In adults, we talk about it as "blanking out", but for children, it is a diagnosis of ADHD.

And for the ADHD child, the classroom represents the heat of battle. The Nintendo game represents performance after the emotions have cooled off. Just because a child's cognitive ability is preempted by anger or anxiety, it most certainly does not mean he has a neurological defect or disability.

Emotions and Rational Decisions

Smoking is a good adult example of how emotions subvert the most well intended rational intentions.

Everyone knows the dangers of smoking. There are frequent articles decrying smoking in all manners of periodicals. Most smokers can articulate this well. But when deep in the throes of a nicotine fit (i.e., negative emotional arousal), the smoker's rationale, knowledge, training, beliefs, intentions are overpowered by the craving for nicotine.

This desperate need for a nicotine fix drives behavior; the fragile cognitive processes don't. So the smoking goes on. The smoking persists despite the rational, mental acknowledgment that smoking is hazard-ous to one's health and perhaps even fatal.

These same arguments apply to other dysfunctional behaviors — such as obesity, alcoholism, child abuse, or stress.

Similarly, emotional responses also wreak havoc on the child's ability to follow through on rational intentions and agreements with others. If simple cognitive knowledge and choices do not change these negative choices in adults, how can we expect like strategies to change ADHD behavior? That is essentially what we are expecting of children when we talk to them about their "bad choices" to punch a friend, hop around the room, or not do their work.

What consequences can a child's "bad choices" have that compare with the potentially fatal choices adults make? If adults cannot control their own emotionally driven behavior, how can we expect it of children?

The only difference is power. Adults have the power to impose strategies on children. If children cannot make these ill conceived strategies work, then adults have the power to impose diagnoses on children and drug them.

Once a child is emotionally aroused by, say, a parent's words, a math book, or a teacher (as opposed to a craving for a cigarette), it is almost impossible for him to access logical abilities. The quiet and fragile insights and persuasive arguments that he has appreciated, understood, and agreed to are inaccessible because of emotional arousal. Emotions rather than reason are dictating action. This is often labeled impulsiveness and irresponsibility rather than emotionally driven behavior.

To deal with this impulsive behavior, the underlying emotions must be extinguished. Once negative emotions are extinguished, then cognitive understanding and resolve are much more likely to control behavior.

Clinically, the causal link between the anger and anxiety and the academic performance deficits are very clear. When this anger is extinguished by Computer Aided Emotional Restructuring, these children can perform as well in the classroom as in Nintendo. The child moves from a state of anger and anxiety to one of ability to attend normally — where he can access the same intellectual capabilities he possesses while playing Nintendo.

What You Say May Not be What They Hear

The lightning speed of the ADHD child's emotional responses to instructions often preempts what a parent or teacher says. The parent says, "Clean up your room." But before the parent finishes saying the word "clean," the child is furious.

That's because this interaction has a history. The child has a conditioned emotional response to the parent's voice, tone and words. That response is to his feelings of anger, rather than his parent's instruction to clean up his room. Indeed, the response is so strong that the full request is barely, if at all, heard. The child then acts on his feelings of anger, rather than the merits of the parental request.

This conditioned emotional response blocks, or at least delays, the intellectual evaluation of the instruction. This conflict and emotional arousal is difficult, not only for the adults but also for the child. Some children learn to avoid much of it, particularly in the classroom, by learning attentional avoidance of the whole experience.

Susan, an 8-Year-Old ADHD Girl

Susan was an 8-year-old, white female who had a long history of unsuccessful treatment for ADHD. This included parent training, behavior modification, and many years on Ritalin. These approaches had some short-term, positive effect. But as time passed, her behavior worsened. When I first met her in August 1992, her medication had been discontinued for several months due to its ineffectiveness.

By the time I began treating Susan, she was very agitated, hostile, antagonistic, and hyperactive. She was constantly wiggling, moving around the room, impulsively interrupting conversations, acting out with outbursts of anger, playing roughly with other children, and showing poor attention span — characterized by moving from task to task every few moments.

She constantly provoked adults around her, particularly her mother. Any comment or instruction from her mother roused Susan to explode before her mother could stop speaking. Her boredom tolerance was nominal, compliance was minimal, and she never stopped moving.

Initial treatment with CAER was difficult because of her limited attention span. Every few moments she would ask questions, sit up in the chair, or ask to do something else. Within the first treatment hour, the behavior subsided. She began to attend for five or six minutes, uninterrupted.

On succeeding sessions, she listened to a tape of her mother giving her directions, which typically provoked her misbehavior, or remembered times at school that made her angry. Initially these procedures caused strong emotional responses including yelling, grimaces, hand waving and wiggling. After several repetitions, the emotional arousal quieted to relaxation.

Susan's mother noted significant improvements at home and school by the third session. By the sixth session, no further problem behaviors could be identified. Her mother related that Susan's behavior had been very good at both school and home. She said that Susan is "calmer, minds better, attends better, and her behavior has changed 180 degrees." Her compliance with mother's requests no longer roused angry outbursts and they were often obeyed without comment. Her attention was quite normal. In a conversational setting, she now sat calmly, made continuous eye contact, and listened.

But by the end of treatment (seven sessions), Susan could attend continuously to CAER for 15 minutes or more without complaining and with no noticeable breaks in attention or superfluous bodily movement. Her general presentation was that of a normal, well-behaved child.

Watching Susan play with other children in the waiting room revealed a normal child capable of playing well, sharing toys, and sustaining interaction. Other children seemed to enjoy her too.

Her mother was also treated on CAER. The primary focus was on the ways her daughter irritated her. Treatment for the mother substantially reduced the negative reactions she had towards her daughter. Their positive interactions were greatly improved.

At four months follow-up, no regression was reported in either mother or daughter.

Chapter 7

Attentional Patterns and Behavior

Critical Timing of Coercion and Avoidance in the Conditioned Attentional Avoidance Loop Model: Slow Speed of Avoidance Learning vs. Fast Speed for Punishment

People learn much more quickly from punishment than from positive reinforcement. The combination of these consequences for behavior can be destructive when it involves the interaction of two people such as a teacher and a student, as we will see.

This interlocking pattern between teacher and student occurs because punishment acts almost instantly, but the punishment is ultimately weak in effect.

By contrast, learning bolstered by positive reinforcement takes much longer to materialize, but it is ultimately more powerful and stable.

When children are motivated by punishment, though, their first response is to do better, to cease acting out, or get back to work. This encourages the teacher to use punishment again.

The child, however, eventually learns how to do a better job of spacing out and ignoring the teacher. Therefore, the teacher, to get the child to do what he wants, has to resort to more severe punishment.

Then, once again, the child is stimulated to learn more effective attentional avoidance, and so on, each taking a turn at demonstrating a more intense version of their coping strategy to the other.

This is apparent in the increasing desperation and effort in the teacher or parent and the degenerating behavior in the child. Both, in their own way, are spinning further and further out of control.

Willful vs. Conditioned Attention

The distinction between conditioned and willful control of attention needs some elaboration because it is not one we normally think about.

Conditioned control is a combination of two things—

1) Conditioned attention to important stimuli

2) Conditioned avoidance of irrelevant and some-times fiercely unpleasant stimuli – as explained above

In contrast, willful attention control is that effortful attention we deliberately and consciously focus.

There is always a balance between willful and conditioned control. But because we usually think of our attention being strictly under our own willful control, the idea of conditioned focus of attention may seem foreign.

Part of the reason we do not think about our conditioned attention patterns is because they are effortless and automatic. Only when these patterns become a problem do we become aware of them. In fact, most of our attention is directed automatically through learned complex patterns.

Willful Attention

We identify ourselves with the mental action of willful attention because it gives us our sense of purpose and direction.

Willful attention is how we teach ourselves new skills. It is the same attention that one uses at the dance studio to mechanically control one's dance steps and say, "One, two, three. One, two, three. One, two, three."

This tedious, slow, purposeful direction of behavior and thoughts serves as the initial patterning for the development of many new skills. It is how we train our automatic processes.

The willful mind takes the body through the pattern repeatedly until the pattern can be elicited as a whole with little effort. Then the pattern becomes known, for example, as the fox trot rather than one, two, three, one, two, three. We can never dance well until the dance steps are turned into automatic behavioral sequences. In fact, the majority of our activities, including our ability to focus our attention are automatically conditioned patterns. Willful attention is a very limited resource that must be maximally conserved by transferring as many activities to conditioned attention as possible.

In addition, willful attention has severely limited capabilities. We can barely do any task more complex than the one, two, three used for learning a new dance. The main purpose of willful attention is to trigger or inhibit response sequences that have already been automated.

Yet, we grossly overestimate the power of willful attention and its power to control our behavior. Willful attention is analogous to the cursor on a computer screen. It is a small point at which we can make an intensive, precise change. However, it is the only point in the computer's massive power that we control directly. The rest of the computer goes its way doing what it has been taught to do, working diligently in our behalf, quietly and unseen.

Like the computer cursor, willful attention is used to train automatic behavior patterns. Through willful attention, we potentially have the power to shape the automatic processes to serve our willful choices. But like programming the computer, this is a slow, systematic process with rewards that accumulate over time.

Whether the process is focused on learning calculus, basketball, or meditation, willful attention works the same. Change progresses in small, systematic, repetitious steps toward establishing an automatic mental pattern, not by means of continuously using willful choices to cause the behavior we want to happen.

This picture of the role of willful attention poses a sharp contrast to the demands we regularly try to make on it. We act as though we can change complex, long-standing patterns of behavior the same way we change our dance step from one, two, three to one, two, three, four. That type of direct, willful change is only possible for simple motor behaviors.

We falsely assume that one can apply this model of willful control of motor behavior to more complex behaviors. That is an impossible demand. The illusion that we can willfully demand control of long-standing behavior patterns only leads to frustration. To change conditioned behaviors, one must change the emotions that drive them rather than trying to ask the child to make "better choices."

Conditioned Attention

A professional basketball player puts conditioned attention into play when he notices, with a quick scan of the court, where all the players are, what they are doing, what the court conditions are, what the ball feels like, and what his coach is doing.

He uses conditioned attention when he ignores (inhibits) the crowd noise and the bright lights. And all of this he does automatically and effortlessly. He is not aware of going down some mental checklist of choices of things to keep track of or to ignore. It is only when something goes wrong with these conditioned patterns that willful attention takes over.

That's when he efficiently blends his willful attention with his conditioned attention.

For the athlete, the intrusion that causes him to slip out of conditioned attention and move into willful attention may be an instruction from the coach. For the ADHD child, the intrusion may be an order from the teacher. Both pull the person out of automatic mode for a moment.

As any teacher, parent, or coach can testify, the child's brief willful attention to this interruption is likely to have little effect on his overall behavior pattern. That's because behavior patterns are easy to interrupt, but they are nearly impossible to change with simple instruction. One, two, three, one, two, three. Repetition is one way of changing behavior patterns. Throw lay-up after lay-up after lay-up. This is the reason we have practices and homework.

But another way to change patterns is to extinguish the emotional cues that trigger and maintain behaviors.

Changing Attentional Patterns is Not Like Sports Practice

Unfortunately, for the ADHD child, athletic practices and homework do not repattern integrated response sequences in the same way. There is a core motivational difference between these two situations. Children go out for sports and participate in practices because it is fun. They are seldom forced. So, aversion is seldom part of the picture.   If practices stop being fun, performance deteriorates and the child usually quits the sport.

Though we tend to treat homework and school work like athletic practices, they come from a very different motivational base. Children do not choose to be in school because it is fun. If school ceases to be fun, performance tends to deteriorate, but the child usually cannot quit.

Aversive tasks and consequences are very much part of the academic learning situation. Children are forced to continue extended, regular contact with the aversive situations — school and homework. The same forces that caused the initial decline in performance at the un-fun point continue to degrade the student's performance. And as the student continues to collect un-fun experiences associated with school, his performance worsens even more.

What this means is that ADHD students do learn a great deal by their continued contact with educational tasks. It is just not what we wanted them to learn. They, like the child who goes out for a sport, learn to optimize fun and minimize un-fun.

In an environment that is primarily motivated by punishment (this is not meant as a criticism of school but just as a statement of how these children experience it), this optimization means escaping the aversive experience by learning attentional avoidance. We call this skill ADHD, which is not what was planned but, given the contingencies and following the learning model, exactly what one would expect.

Ultimately, it is very difficult to force people to perform well on tasks they don't like, but that is what we try to do with students in school. We provide them with a special teacher to continue rehearsing tasks that they don't like, we give them more homework to practice tasks that are beyond unpleasant to them, and we give them after school tutoring programs to rehearse courses that trigger responses in them that they can't control.

Unless these practices are qualitatively different, like Nintendo, what will be learned is finely tuned attentional avoidance. This is why these programs so often fail.

To be successful, these programs need to present the students with qualitatively different stimuli, such as a very charismatic teacher, a different situation, or different motivational systems — not more of the same.

The Shifting Conditioned-Willful Attentional Balance

The child's miserably unpleasant situation — school — continues every day, six hours per day, year in and year out. This provides a tremendous amount of opportunity and motivation to practice attentional avoidance. Though he probably consciously wants to attend to the appropriate tasks, at a more powerful, emotional level, against his will, his mind is being shaped in the opposite direction. His attentional avoidance becomes extremely well trained and automatic, to the point of being out of the ADHD child's willful consciousness and control. It becomes more automated and out of consciousness than fingernail chewing. He is on auto-pilot.

ADHD Auto-pilot

This auto-pilot experience is not unique to these children. We all experience it from time to time.

I can remember one Saturday morning when I climbed into my car to do some errands. As I was heading for the store, I began thinking about ideas to include in this book. The next thing I knew, I was pulling into my parking place at my office.

How had I gotten there without knowing it? I had traveled for over ten miles of a complex route with traffic. Like many people on their way to work, I was on auto-pilot, and my auto-pilot was set for the office. I did not do it intentionally; several cues automatically put me in that mode.

Initially the route going anywhere from my house is the same. Only after a distance, do the routes to different places diverge. This means that the cues I was experiencing while intending to go to the store were the same cues I would experience if I were going to my office. I was simply following a chain. Once this chain was operating, I followed succeeding links because nothing interfered.

Also, I was thinking about the kinds of things that I do when I am at work. Since I was mentally preoccupied, as the ADHD child is, I went into auto-pilot until I found myself at work. I followed deeply conditioned patterns and responses.

This is exactly what the ADHD child does, except that I ended up at work. The child ends up in the back of the classroom with his hand in the fish tank.

This happens to the ADHD child because his conditioning is more difficult to interrupt since it is highly over-learned and driven by anger and anxiety.

As the Conditioned Attentional Avoidance Loop Model explains, the ADHD child's reactions accelerate. They become stronger, more efficient, quicker, more complete, and more exaggerated. The attentional breaks become so profound that the ADHD child can no longer exert much willful control over his behavior.

And the conditioned attentional patterns of ADHD children begin to include less and less of the child's immediate surroundings. When this level of attentional avoidance is reached, his behavior begins to reflect this avoidance. Although the child cognitively understands the social expectancy for sitting in his seat, he can no longer willfully attend to and act upon this demand.

The child is responding to natural, emotionally driven impulses for escape by moving around the classroom, impulsively speaking out in class, and generally acting hyperactive – behavior commonly associated with these children.

And, he is reacting to the impulses as they strike him at the moment with little cognitive inhibition of those impulses to bring them within socially accepted limits.

He simply can't break out of this auto-pilot mode.

Conjuring Rational Answers to "Why"

If you ask me or the ADHD child why I drove on auto-pilot to the office on Saturday, or why did he put his hand in the fish tank, the correct answer is almost always the same — I don't know.

If pressured for a better answer, the ADHD child can conjure up an explanation that will satisfy your way of thinking. But the child is giving you such an answer simply because he wants to please you. And in this situation the "right" answer pleases, but it is not correct. It's not correct because the answer is created after-the-fact and does not represent what really happened.

If you truly listen to an ADHD child rather than demand to know "why," his honest answer is that he doesn't know why. There was no premeditation on his part. He was on auto-pilot, just like I was on auto-pilot while driving to the office.

There are two levels to this after-the-fact, introspective explanation of the forces working within him, i.e. the why. The child's "I don't know" answer is the first level and often points to the gaps in his experience. He steps into the second level when you press him with more ambiguous questions, "What was happening with you?"

This slide from level one to level two is quick and smooth. Typically it goes something like this:

The teacher catches the child behaving inappropriately and asks, "Why did you do that?"

He doesn't know the reason any more than the teacher does. Again, the truth really is "I don't know." He just found himself doing it.

But the child answers, "I didn't hear you." Or, he says, "I didn't see him."

Translation: I was "checked out."

Incredulous, the adult says, "I said it three times." Or, "What? You couldn't miss him."

In desperation the child replies, "You said I could." Or, "He hit me first."

The more negative the feedback the child gets at the first stage, the faster he escalates to the second stage of true conjuring.

On the second level, when you ask him more open ended, less demanding questions he reveals the emotions driving his behavior, emotions such as fear, anger, frustration, anxiety or guilt. He may say things like "This stuff is dumb," "I'm bored," "I can't do it anymore," or "Who cares." Children also describe this state as suddenly finding themselves standing in the back of the classroom pushing someone or speaking out without permission.

The children's ability to generate answers to why, gives us a mistaken sense of validation that their behaviors come out of cognitive choices. Believing that they have hit on a solution, these misguided teachers and parents continue talking to the child about making "bad choices."

In a sense, both the adult and child are cooperating to maintain this shared deception. The child complies because he is motivated to please adults, not a desire to irritate adults or to be a "space cadet."

The Limitations of Willful Control of Behavior

Our notion that behavior is directed by rational thinking is culturally instilled. Our daily experience is in sharp contrast to this cultural dogma. Anyone who has ever been told "You shouldn't be mad at him." or "Just forget about it." knows what I am talking about. The inference is that I can change how I feel just as I change the position of my arm. Motor movements and emotions are at the extreme opposite ends of the willful control continuum.

Essentially, feelings are involuntary, conditioned responses, much like our pulse. We have almost as little willful control over our pulse rate as we do our feelings. But conditioning, rather than willing, can change our pulse as well as our emotions. If we want to change our emotional response we have to proceed just like a dog trainer does in dog obedience class. Good emotions need to be repeatedly and systematically reinforced and destructive ones extinguished.

The ADHD child's conflict between what he knows he should do and what he actually does is not unique to him. Most of us eat things that we clearly know we should not, be it a fattening slab of beef, alcohol, or a cookie. How is it that we go ahead, do things that we clearly know we should not, and may even tell others that they should not either?

We constantly hear people say things like, "I don't know why I do...," "I can't seem to help myself from doing ...," "I find my self doing ... when I know I shouldn't." It sounds as if there are two people living in the same body, one that knows what should be done and one that does whatever has been automatically conditioned. This is strikingly similar to the ADHD child's predicament. Whatever defect the ADHD child has, it appears that we all have it too.

As has been repeatedly argued above, ADHD children are not very different from the rest of us. Primarily, medical language and diagnostic fervor frame them as being different and defective. They are not bad kids. Like other children, they really want to please. Most of the younger ones are very good-humored.

In the initial stages, ADHD children really want to pay attention but can't. Later they become overtly angry and resentful because of the immense amount of negative feedback they receive from everyone. Attentional avoidance of this aversiveness is only partially successful, so they still and sometimes act out anger towards their perceived tormentors.

Chapter 8

ADHD and Anger

Cultural Contradiction Both Promotes and Controls Anger

There are cadres of individual entrepreneurs who profit from marketing products that exploit the entertainment value of anger. These products include violent movies, sports, video games, music, TV, and books.

On the other side, the agents of the larger cultural good — such as government, churches, schools, or community organizations — attempt to control anger.

These opposing cultural forces set up an internal conflict in the individual. The struggle between these two forces has high physical, emotional, and cultural costs.

Ellen Goodman, columnist from the Boston Globe says it well:

> *Americans once expected parents to raise their children in accordance with the dominant cultural messages. Today they are expected to raise their children in opposition to them. Once the chorus of cultural values was full of ministers, teachers, neighbors, and leaders. They demanded more conformity, but offered more support. Now the messengers are violent cartoon characters, rappers and celebrities selling sneakers. Parents are considered responsible only if they are successful in their resistance. That's what makes child raising harder. It's not just that American families have less time with their kids; it's that we have to spend more of this time doing battle with our own culture.*

What We Consider "Fun"

If you really look at what our culture promotes as entertainment or fun, it is pretty appalling. We pay money to see murder, mayhem, theft, assault, vulgarity, sociopathology, anger, boxing, violent sports like football and hockey and so on.

Since we are willing to pay money to experience this anger and aggression, we must consider them reinforcing emotions. We must enjoy them.

The latest and most sought after variation on these vicarious thrills is virtual reality, which can feel very real. This new computer technology moves us significantly along the dimension from passive to active participation in revolting forms of entertainment.

About all that is missing from participation in these first quality virtual reality participation activities is personal harm. If adults are willing to pay money to participate vicariously or virtually in socially undesirable behavior, why shouldn't children also find these behaviors reinforcing?

This is precisely the position of the frustrated child in the classroom. They are at liberty to enjoy not just the virtual, but the full living entertainment derived from whatever chaos they can cause because, in a way, it is a virtual experience.

Because of the synthetic nature of the classroom, their experience of personal harm is precluded (even though there is an obvious natural consequence of some of their behavior). Like high-tech virtual reality experiences, they can enjoy the entertainment without fear of harm, at least physically.

Quite accurately, they sometimes tell authority figures, "You can't make me." The classroom is a low-tech version of virtual reality entertainment, and the ADHD child is its patron.

If you look at boys' play, it is apparent why boys are far over-represented (2:1) in the diagnosis of ADHD. For fun, boys fight, wrestle, play "Star Wars", warfare, play football, box, and so forth.

By contrast girls gossip, play dolls and dress-up.

Obviously, the angry, aggressive, and anti-social twist on entertainment is more of "a man thing."

Anger as a Part of ADHD

Anger has a number of sources for the ADHD child: the cultural anger mentioned above, the negative feedback of being labeled, male aggression, slower male development, and conflicting social values.

The Conditioned Attentional Avoidance Loop Model & the Development of Anger

The Conditioned Attentional Avoidance Loop Model describes an early and precipitating stage of development of ADHD, particularly the characteristic abnormal attentional patterns themselves.

First, anxiety is avoided by attentional avoidance. This causes the environment to become more aggressive in its attempts to demand compliance with cultural expectations. The most common strategy the environment uses to induce compliance is punishment because punishment provides the quickest reinforcement for the one doing the punishing.

Punishment reflexively elicits an angry response from the target (be it a person or a laboratory rat), in this case the ADHD child. Thus, anger becomes an important element in the child's exchange with the environment.

And anger begets more anger.

One can see this anger grow as ADHD children get older. Young ADHD children are usually fairly happy, pleasant children. As they grow older, they become more hostile, aggressive, and unpleasant to be around. By adolescence, they are often hostile, acting out, and in conflict with authority.

Why More Boys Get ADHD

Matt was first brought to my office after shoving and kicking another child in a hallway confrontation. While reviewing the incident on CAER, he first described the feeling preceding the incident with a growling yell. He was able to trace that growling feeling back to a time his big brother had beat up on him and a time when he had been bullied on the school grounds by some older kids. He finally described the feeling as fear rather than anger.

Apparently the incident had been triggered by a rush of fear because he thought the kid he had kicked and shoved was accompanied by some friends who were going to beat Matt up. Actually, the other boys were not with the victim, but because of his fear, Matt thought they were. He attacked in an attempt to keep from getting beat up like he had been in the past.

Male Aggression: Social Role Conflict for Boys

Our culture is often inconsistent in its demands on the individual. There is no place this conflict of social role more clearly demonstrated than in the demands we place on boys. On the one hand, we want them to be compliant, polite, sensitive and achieving. On the other hand, we want them to be assertive, aggressive, stand up for what they believe in, fight for what is theirs, and to "not take any crap" from anyone. Boys are supposed to challenge the system, but not too much.

We also seem to think there is something cute about boys who are always "into something," who are macho, spunky, or aggressive. The newspaper cartoon "Dennis the Menace* " is a classic example of our enjoying the idea that "boys will be boys."

"WHO SAYS THERE'S NO SUCH THING AS *PERPETUAL MOTION?*"

Boys are required to make some very skilled judgments about when aggression is appropriate and when it is negatively sanctioned.

Years ago, when our culture was less crowded, less demanding, and less medicalized, young male aggression was passed off as "just having a little fun." Now, this very same aggression is seen as an illness.

Yesterday's boys risked a spanking; today's boys risk being diagnosed and drugged. At the peril of being accused of advocating child abuse, I think spanking (not a beating) is more humane than diagnosing and drugging. A spanking may hurt more today, but in the long run what the child learns about himself and the world around him may be less damaging.

With a medical diagnosis and Ritalin, the message is "I am wrong (defective)." With a moral judgment and a spanking, the message is "I did wrong." The supposition that follows such a message is, I have a chance of controlling what I do. There is nothing I can do about what I am.

Slower Development of Boys

Boys also run into more frustrations as they confront the structured demands of school. Their slower physical, emotional, and intellectual development make early school more difficult for them. They suffer more failure experiences and more negative feedback, both for their lower performance and for their more aggressive natures.

This provides more opportunities for ADHD to begin.

Chapter 9

Metamorphosis of Anger in ADHD

Human achievement is largely a product of cooperative group effort. This is how we built pyramids, space shuttles, and New York City. If we didn't cooperate, social, intellectual, and material achievements would not be possible.

Because of this social utility of cooperation, one of the main agendas of any culture is to control interpersonal aggression and anger. One of the ways we achieve the behavior patterns conducive to cooperation is by managing anger in less destructive ways.

Ideally, beginning in childhood, we "metamorphose" anger into other processes.

Metamorphosis of Anger from Behavior to ADHD

For the ADHD child, the metamorphosis of anger goes through three sequential stages, which negatively trigger each other.

First, annoying behavior is translated into a personal characteristic of the child, anger. Second, translating it into thoughts controls the anger. Finally, the thinking problem, that is, attentional avoidance, is translated into a medical problem, ADHD.

From Behavior to Personal Trait

The first step is the translation of the offending behavior, from what is initially just an annoying behavior, into a characteristic of the child. At first, he is simply instructed not to yell, hit, or run. There is little mention of the feeling that might be involved.

After repeated episodes, we begin to think of the behavior as chronic and characteristic of the child. We suggest to the child that he is angry, which is likely true. The ADHD child may be asked, "Why are you angry?" The subtle, but important point is that the child is no longer just misbehaving, the child is now thought of as having a problem, anger.

Once the child has a problem, the strategy for controlling it moves from simply acting on the behavior to a higher level of abstraction and intervention. Now, we not only punish the child for the misbehavior, but we also address his anger at an abstract and symbolic level.

This is the beginning of the very subtle and powerful process of anger alchemy, which finally ends with the development of the behavior and diagnosis of ADHD.

Anger Alchemy

When the child's anger becomes too unpleasant for the adult, then there is an attempt to control it. And since the "problem" is now referenced by this abstract verbal construct — anger — it is open to a variety of verbal maneuvers.

We teach our children three strategies to control their anger:

1)   We turn their angry feelings into thoughts.

2)   We trigger a shift from an emotional state to a cognitive one.

3)   We shift the responsibility for the feeling of anger from ourselves to the child.

We thus guide how our children learn to think and talk about angry feelings.   And we do this to protect ourselves, as well as the culture, from our children's anger.

Children whose behavior is seen as driven by thought are easier to control than those who are seen as driven by feeling. Thoughts are considered more agreeable to work with than emotions. And that's because we believe we have a greater sense of control over thoughts. We apply different procedures to controlling thoughts than we do to feelings.   Therefore, pretending that angry feelings are really thoughts makes them more amenable to the logical tools of self-control.

Language is the tool we use to manipulate our thoughts. Since our culture does not tolerate the display of anger and its variants, we use language to shape the way children describe and experience their feelings.   In other words, we require ADHD children to speak in terms of cognitively diluted descriptions of their emotional experience.

For example, one can hear the parent of an obviously angry child reviewing his "choices" with him, or using phrases such as, "You are just having a problem right now; we can fix the toy later."

The angry feeling is translated into a logical issue called a problem, and that problem can be solved with choices.   The redefining of the feeling as a problem then allows us to apply the cognitive tools of problem solving.

The repetition of similar rephrasing eventually teaches the child the words he can say that will get us to listen. These words slowly shift the focus of the problem from physical feeling (emotion) to a dry, abstract thought.

The issue is not whether such strategies are good or bad. Rather, understanding the mechanisms the culture uses allows us to adjust, modify, and supplement these strategies so that we maximize the benefits and minimize the costs.

This, and the next technique, sidestep the issue of emotional-physiological arousal.

By teaching children to search for the exact word to best describe their experience, we force them again to shift out of an emotional state into the cognitive state. This is the second tool.

Instead of "anger," we use words like annoyance, hostility, jealousy, frustration, and contempt. We like to think of these words as providing a more precise description of the feeling. That may be true, but that is not the major function of word discrimination.

The task is to search actively through all the possible appropriate words, trying each to select the most fitting one. This process requires a shift to a cognitive state. By eliciting a cognitive state, the child's internal state is shifted away from his angry emotional state. And this willfully created cognitive state dilutes the emotional experience and, more importantly, the expression of anger. For this reason, our culture reinforces the use of such language as one more technique to blunt the expression of anger.

The third verbal maneuver of anger alchemy is to blame the child for the problem or, in more politically correct lingo, to make them "take responsibility for" their anger.

Personal change is hard work over an extended period of time. That is the reason we, as human beings, like to blame others for everything that annoys us. Once it is their fault, defect, or problem, then they have to do the work of changing how they are. Change is always a better idea for someone else than it is for ourselves.

One of the subtlest and most effective ways of shifting blame is to shift the language we use to describe the problem. Through carefully selected language, we subtly put the onus for change on children, rather than taking on the responsibility of changing their environment to be less provocative of anger.

Although children are very clear that certain things make them angry, we refuse to listen to what they say is the source of their feelings. By not to responding to the words they use to describe the external source for their anger, we force them to search out language to which we will respond.

By shaping the language they use to communicate their feelings to us, we are, in essence, trying to teach them to internalize these angry feelings.

If a child is obviously angry, we reflect his anger back on him by emphasizing his ownership of his anger. We describe his experience by saying something like, "Looks like YOU hurt yourself." or "Are YOU going to let him make you mad?" We put an emphasis on YOU. YOU change the focus from the experience of the emotion to assigning responsibility for the emotion and for its expression.

Anger is twisted and reframed as the child's defect — rather than the child's attempt to adapt to living in a very anger-provoking world. By cultural dictum, children are supposed to docilely accept and ignore the absurdity of their situation. Compliance is the key word. If you do not comply, you are labeled sick i.e., ADHD.

Please be clear, I am not an advocate of dumping your anger all over everyone. Anger and aggression must be controlled for a culture to survive. I am just explaining the cultural mechanisms for anger control so that we can understand the current methodology for developing cultural cooperation. We need to understand where we are and how we got there before we can craft new ways of managing anger.

The Fiction of Individual Responsibility

If individuals are not individually in control of their emotions, behavior, and physiological changes but are responsive to their current and past social situations, it is a deceptive and ineffective fiction to try to induce the individual "to take responsibility for controlling his feelings." We act as if he has willful control over feelings in the same way he has willful control over the movement of his arm.

The illusion of personal responsibility is seductive because individual action can often solve minor problems. Because we're satisfied with the results for minor, circumscribed problems, we generalize the strategies of personal responsibility to bigger, more chronic or complicated issues. This often does not work.

The notion of rigid responsibility for one's own feelings and behavior is a damaging cultural fiction. It may be neat and convenient, but it does not provide us an effective model upon which to base change strategies.

To resolve this apparent conflict, we must make a distinction between willful control of and responsibility for emotions and behaviors. The fact that an individual cannot change emotions, like he can change the movement of his arm, does not absolve him from taking action to resolve the problem.

The fact that an individual's feelings and behaviors occur in a larger context does not give us license to sidestep personal responsibility. Children often say, "He made me do it." Though there may be much factual truth to this assertion, it should not be used as an excuse for avoiding personal action to resolve the problem.

The action may not be as simple as making a choice. The action is likely to be more complex than individual willful self- control because it will require the cooperation of others. Individuals have to act in concert to take effective responsibility for emotions, just as they did to build pyramids or space shuttles.

If we want ADHD children to manage their anger we must effectively manage their situation in sophisticated and complex ways, rather than just using medical diagnoses to point the finger at them and drug them.

The whole web of contextual determinates of behavior, including the classroom, teacher, school, family, media, etc. must be partly personally responsible for change. It is groups of individuals taking coordinated responsibility and action on these fronts, not isolated individuals each trying to stand against the overwhelming flood of this situational influence that is required for effective and meaningful personal responsibility.

There is a great risk in what I have just said. Individual responsibility is a social belief that has been reinforced not because of its factual truth, but because of its social utility. We use this illusion to get individuals to take action to solve problems. Since groups do not solve problems, and individuals do, for the culture's sake, it is the individual who must feel responsible for action and be motivated to carry it out.

The difference is that the point of responsibility and the point of action are different. He must direct his action not just toward himself, but also toward others in his environment. Our approach must be more sophisticated than blaming.

When the child cannot behaviorally take "responsibility" for his anger, the way he does for the movement of his arm, the inadequacy of the responsibility model becomes clearly apparent. We abandon the responsibility model in favor of its opposite, the medical model.

The application of the medical model, in the form of applying the ADHD diagnosis, absolves both the child and parent of responsibility for his behavior. He now has a neurological problem, which prevents him from being responsible. We can now blame this disease entity within him, Mr. ADHD

The Diagnosis of the ADHD Homunculus

The last step in the metamorphosis into ADHD is the creation of a medical homunculus. The homunculus is a medieval concept of a little man in our head who causes us to do the things we do.

MR. ADHD AT THE CONTROLS

When our clever verbal redirection of the child's anger does not stem his rising academic and behavior problems, the strategy of medical diagnosis is applied. Eventually, the problem behaviors rise to the level of a specific medical entity — ADHD.

The child is no longer responsible for solving his problem; he now has a problem — ADHD. It is a medical problem, just like a cold, and a defect over which he has no more responsibility than he does a cold.

Once the child is absolved of responsibility for his problem, both the child and the adults around him have a joint adversary. They can form an alliance to battle this common, external to them both, enemy — ADHD. Together, they can blame the ADHD homunculus within the child.

This is just as was done with the "demon possessed" during the Dark Ages, only now we have named the homunculus Mr. ADHD. He recites medicaleze, rather than Bible verses, to explain his actions. Changing his name and language does not make him any more plausible or useful as an explanation of human behavior. In essence, the beliefs change over the ages, but the processes stay the same.

This displacement of responsibility can be noted in the statements teachers make about ADHD children. Teachers will sometimes have a little meeting with their class to explain that "Jason has ADHD, so he can't always help the way he acts. We have to help him."

Parents will make similar excuses for his actions with comments such as, "He can't help it, he has ADHD." Translated, this means his willful self cannot do anything about the problem because his body is possessed by ADHD — we have to put up with the tyranny of his body because he is as helpless to deal with it as we are.

It sounds as if there is another willful person in the child, as if the child is truly possessed, and it is that possession inside him who is causing the difficulty.

Conjuring reasons why he either has choice or no choice presupposes cognitive control of behavior, which are both wrong. It is neither a matter of cognitive choice nor physiological determination. Rather, emotional forces control the thoughts and behavior of the ADHD child.

Chapter 10

Boredom Revisited

Anger Becomes Depression: The Meaning of Bored.

By cultural standards, angry feelings are not right and those who have them are not right. Yet the natural response to anger is to express it, which is what children initially do.

Later, under social pressure, the anger is turned on the self, i.e. the child becomes angry at himself for his angry feelings. This causes the child to turn self-punishing words and feelings on himself, which further compounds the problem.

The young child also experiences the punitive, angry input of parents and teachers as annoying pressure to comply with demands — just as anyone else would. But the ADHD child receives so much more of this punitive treatment that it becomes a central focus of his pattern of interaction with others.

Because of the cultural disapproval of angry behavior, as conveyed by peers, parents, and teachers, the ADHD child begins to disapprove of himself. He models the behavior others display toward him (Bandura, 1962). He internalizes and reflects on himself with the exact same words and feelings that have been directed toward him.

He often sees his behavior as a major cause of his mistreatment, but he feels helpless to do anything about it. He becomes his own worst tormentor, which leads to depression.

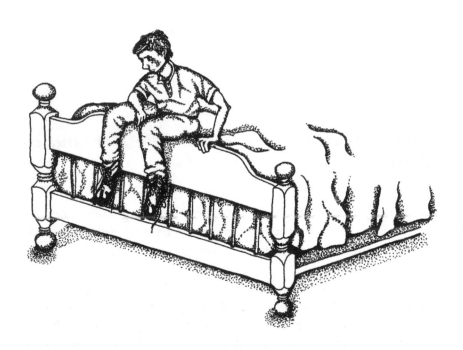

The Good Citizen's Motto: "I'd Rather Depress than Aggress."

Depression is quite apparent in ADHD children. Many of them don't sleep well, some of which is due to stimulant drugs. They can be grumpy and irritable because they are unhappy with themselves and the world around them.

Research using teacher ratings reveals that ADHD students are more depressed than either normal or other children experiencing academic difficulties (Bohline, 1985). Since academic difficulties alone do not result in depression or visa versa, ADHD is obviously connected with depression.

Just as one observes with grown-ups who are depressed, ADHD children are more likely to attribute the causes of both positive and negative events to forces outside themselves (Borden et. al., 1987).

Therefore, from their perspective, the control of their misery or happiness is in the hands of others, and they conclude that nothing they do will make any difference to their fate. Consequently, effort on their part is not relevant since they are helpless to control their lives.

Reading was my first nemesis in school. By second grade, I was being given special help. But as hard as I tried, I stumbled over the few words I knew, and I comprehended nothing. I began to hate the little girls who read so well and who, in my eyes, were the teachers' pets because they read so well. I wanted to punch them out, but I never did.

I felt so incompetent and hopeless. It seemed the harder I tried, the more uptight I got and the poorer I read. I began to outspokenly declare that "I don't need to read. It's not good for anything. It's boring."

Eventually I resented anyone who tried to tutor my reading. My mother spent hours trying to help me, but the whole process made me so frustrated and angry with myself that I fought her all the way. Sometimes, I started crying and ran off because I knew that I would never do as well as those little girls in the class who the teachers so liked to have read out loud.

Failure Expectancies in School: No Positive Reinforcement Schedule

The ADHD child's perception of possible success in school is nil. He sees himself as so far from meeting the standards for reward that it makes no sense to struggle or achieve, from either an emotional or logical level. He begins to form what is referred to as a contrast conception.

In a contrast conception, instead of seeing the similarities between himself and other children, the ADHD becomes highly sensitive to the differences. Specifically, he begins to focus on other children's successes and his own failures, which depresses him further. From his point of view, the gap between his performance and that of others widens until it appears to be an unbridgeable chasm.

The best that the ADHD child believes he can do is blot out the bad feelings. Pain reduction, not academic or social reward, becomes his goal. Since the ADHD child is prohibited from avoidance by physical escape, attentional escape is the only avenue available.

By high school, my grades had begun to improve, but I have two D's on my high school transcript — first and second semester typing.

Dwayne and I were the only boys in this class of more than 30 students. Once a week the teacher had a timed typing test. On Friday, she passed the tests back from best to worst. Those same damn little girls who read so well still got the top honors.

Every week Dwayne and I vied for last and next to the last position. There was no way to slink under my desk when these tests were returned. Every week I had to walk all the way up the front of the class to retrieve my miserable paper. To reconcile ourselves, Dwayne and I used to talk about how boring the class was and how we would never use this anyway.

Underneath the defense, we felt terrible. And it showed when we eventually developed what we called our "alliance with monkeys." (We chose this name because we had heard that enough monkeys typing on enough typewriters for long enough would eventually type out the works of Shakespeare.)

In order to at least not participate in demeaning each other, we resorted to just pounding on our typewriters during the typing test. Since this made both of our tests total garbage, it was random which one of us would be last.

I can still remember the only positive word I ever got from my typing teacher. One day, she complimented me on using the shift lock key rather than holding the shift key. It felt like I had finally done something right. I still sometimes remember that crumb of kindness when I use the shift lock (caps lock) key on my word processor keyboard. I am a little proud that I remembered to use it.

"I'm Bored" Means "I Give Up"

The fact that depressed patients perceive that they are, in a general sense, helpless to change their plight, is not something they have just conjured up. It is an idea they have learned through repeated and ineffective efforts to change the things in their environment that upset them. Over time they also learn to give up all effort to try to change things for the better.

This learning to give up is termed learned helplessness, and it is commonly associated with depression (Seligman, 1975). In fact, learned helplessness has long been considered central to theories of depression and now has been demonstrated experimentally with ADHD children (Milich & Okazaki, 1991). The difference is that ADHD children use another word to explain this same experience. They call it boredom.

Two Meanings of Boredom

Bored is not only the ADHD child's preferred term, in some ways, it is his complaint and retort. Using the term bored is a way of indicating that the adult-generated world out there is boring. Therefore, the problem belongs not to the child but to the world around him. It is his way of passing an insult back to the adult tormentors.

There are two meanings and types of boredom. One builds upon the other.

First, there is the adult sense of boredom that results from under stimulation and is experienced as an emptiness. Children understand this meaning of boredom, but they also use the term to mean something else.

For them, boredom is the aversive, exhausting, hopeless stage, beyond frustration or anger. They feel overwhelmed by the academic and behavioral demands made upon them and incapable of rising to meet them. To them, their situation is hopeless. The feeling is not that of nothingness, in the same way an adult might use the term.

Rather, it is a unique feeling just like anxiety or anger, and it is just as negative. When the child has attempted a task over and over and can't say "shove it" or can't escape physically, when he is to the point of hopelessness, giving up, and being disengaged, then he says, "I'm bored."

How Boredom Works ... for ADHD Kids

There are three reasons ADHD children use the word "bored" to describe their experience. First, there is some similarity between depression and what adults call boredom. Both are painful, a response to external stimulus, and lead to disengagement.

Second, and perhaps more important, adults initially respond more positively to the word bored than to other descriptors — such as angry, mad, or "I hate it." In fact, every parent wants to think of their child as smarter than most. When problems begin to develop, but are still not well defined, it is more appealing for parents to think of their child as really bright but bored with the plebeian activities offered him by his unenlightened (or worse) teacher.

The problem is the teacher and school, not their child. And it is the school's problem to pack the freight for change. Remember, it is a human axiom that it is always better to have someone else do the work of changing.

So, a version of "group-think" sets in. The child who talks about boredom reinforces the idea to the parent. Parental language about boredom likewise reinforces the child's use of the word bored. They have a shared and mutually reinforced conceptual reality — the child's problem is best thought of as boredom.

Third, the idea of being bored with something gives one a sense of superiority over it. For example, being bored with school gives the child a sense of ego support over the very thing that has been so damaging to his ego. This is a clever reframing of negative stimuli into a positive one.

Again, the child's approach is a sophisticated, short-term adaptation, not a disability. This strategy also provides further rationale for the ADHD child to distance himself from school and schoolwork. Such children often develop a life quite separate from school, be it in joining the street culture or simply dropping out.

Sometimes they are quite articulate in differentiating themselves from school. Their message is "Why do I need school?," "That stuff doesn't make a difference," "I'll just get a job." These children just block off the realities involved in living these strategies simply by extending the skills that they used to block off math class. Until and unless the ADHD child's attentional avoidance pattern is extinguished, it is infinitely extendible into other parts of his life on into adulthood.

The Trap in Defining Boredom in the Adult Sense of the Word for ADHD

There is a trap in the use of the word bored by children, and many helpers have fallen into it. The traditional interpretation of boredom implies that there is something lacking and, thus, something must be added to fill the boredom. The belief is that as a result of this addition, the child will become intellectually engaged.

This is a reflection of our "more is better" solution to problems. The temptation is to add a tutor, summer school, extracurricular studies, and the like.

Inherently, there is nothing wrong with these strategies if they are not pressing on bruises. However, with the ADHD child, there is a problem. If the so-called boredom is caused by the first presentation of these strategies, then re-confronting the child with more of the same is going to aggravate, not improve, the situation, no matter how much those skills being taught are needed.

Only after the emotional reactions to these strategies are erased can many children benefit from such opportunities.

Chapter 11

ADHD in Adults

Adult forms of ADHD are now recognized and labeled ADHD/R (residual), whereas it used to be thought that children grew out of ADHD. Research indicates that the adult life of an ADHD person typically includes unstable employment, tumultuous and multiple relationships, as well as depression.

Scott ADHD/R

Scott, a 34-year-old construction superintendent, spent much of his time yelling at his workers. He was explosive and had come too close to being violent with his subordinates. He was divorced from a short, angry marriage. Despite his reports of this angry behavior, his presentation to me was calm, articulate, and cordial. He was clearly intelligent and socially skilled.

But in school, Scott had done poorly, had had many fights, and had barely graduated. Back then he carried a diagnosis of Attention Deficit Disorder (now ADHD).

On CAER, Scott initially focused on one of his recent outbursts. He was asked to remember each incident and re-experience the feelings that went before and during the outburst. Once he found the feelings, he was asked to follow those feelings across his life "like a bloodhound would follow the scent on a sock."

He traced these feelings, which he variously described as angry, jumpy, and frightened, to his earliest school days. He could remember that same feeling when, as a schoolboy, he was unable to meet the demands of teachers. He had extensive recollections of incidents with teachers, peers, and family members that elicited similar feelings.

His current explosions had emotional roots going all the way back to his earliest school experiences. Current situations would subconsciously remind Scott of situations in school. Typically, these early school memories were colored with feelings of frustrations, anger, and threats.

So, whenever Scott was asked to do a task that he doubted he was competent to perform, it reminded him of one of those school situations. And he responded by exploding and attempting to make it look as if it were the other person's problem, just as he did in school.

On CAER, he went over these images until they were difficult to pay attention to and elicited no affect. They became just dry, boring memories.

Within the first three sessions, the explosions had stopped. Two more sessions were used to extinguish what he called a "jumpy-jumpy feeling," which he associated with an impending outburst.

Two-year follow up indicates no regression to his aggressive behavior or the jumpy feeling.

Chapter 12

Current Explanations of ADHD:
Fallacies in Logic

The Nintendo Syndrome: Situational Specificity of ADHD

Despite the ADHD child's usual "boredom," most therapists and parents of these children note the ADHD child's ability to play computer games like Nintendo for hours with no gap in attention. Obviously, this is in direct contrast to their normal ADHD inattention.

Some people — such as reinforcement fading theorists — believe this is because Nintendo has a great variety of novel reinforcers. Not so.

Though Nintendo provides many immediate, short-term reinforcers, it is very repetitious and actually lacks novel reinforcers, particularly since most children play the same game dozens of times. In fact, many of these children have the game memorized to the minutest detail, which is the direct opposite of novelty. So, the novelty explanation of children's attention to Nintendo does not make sense.

What Nintendo does offer is a fantasy environment that is not associated with punishment. Nothing in

Nintendo is similar to their school or homework environment. I know of no children who, prior to learning Nintendo, have any experience with karate kicking, superhero plumbers.

In Nintendo, there are no teachers, no assignments, no desks to sit in, no tests, and no other kids to laugh at you. Since the child's learned, attentional avoidance patterns are not triggered by Nintendo, the child attends quite normally. (In my day, reading hot-rod magazines was the equivalent.)

In other words, it is a world that bears little resemblance to the child's daily reality — adult involvement, academic cues, or skill demands. There is little association between daily life experience and the computer game world.

Conditioned Attentional Avoidance Loop Model theory allows us to shift our focus away from an attention deficit in the ADHD child to learned performance anxiety cues, which are the key to the problem and its solution.

Children, therefore, can be successful in situations such as Nintendo because they are not touching any historically conditioned performance anxiety cues and because this fantasy environment offers clear, achievable steps toward success.

ADHD CHRONICLE 25¢

Mario karate kicks reinforcement fading theory into oblivion... Provides insight into how Computer Aided Emotional Restructuring works for ADHD kids!

The Nintendo Syndrome

The Nintendo syndrome is apparent in other novel situations. Take, for example, an ADHD child in a one-to-one situation like a visit to the doctor. The credibility of many parents has been impugned when they take their ADHD child to the pediatrician. When the doctor interviews the child, the child is a perfect gentleman, without a sign of any ADHD behaviors. The conclusion is that "it must be something the parents are doing."

More accurately, the difference in the child's behavior is that the doctor does not have a history with the child.

To understand the difficulties of ADHD children, one must have data from a variety of different situations. An office examination can be very misleading and data taken primarily from such situations leads to an under-diagnosis.

Conversely, an over-diagnosis will result from data taken primarily from a parent. Professional evaluation requires an insightful evaluation of data from all sources.

A Fancy Test Does Not a Pathology Make

A variety of very sophisticated testing procedures have been developed to test for ADHD, as well as to look at the neurological mechanisms that theoretically underlie these problems.

There is a certain magic about how a measurement procedure can make a concept seem more real. If you are talking about concrete things that you can measure with a yardstick, then that imparts an element of truth.

But it is dangerous to generalize this strategy to invisible concepts. That's because the yardsticks do not measure what they are supposed to measure. The attractiveness of testing is still seductive, particularly if these measurements confirm some pet theory describing the underlying phenomenon.

In this desire for closure lies a logical trap. First, let's look at some of the research used to point to physiological bases for ADHD; then we will look at the flaws in this logic.

Physiological Cues: PET Studies

Adherents of the physiological basis for ADHD are fond of citing Positron Emission Tomography (PET) studies. PET uses radio labeled glucose to measure local changes in metabolism in different parts of the brain. Such studies show about an eight percent lower metabolism of glucose in the brains of ADHD adults during continuous performance tasks (Zametkin et al., 1990).

This metabolic reduction was the greatest in the prefrontal and premotor regions of the brain. From other studies of patients with injuries or lesions, it is known that these frontal areas serve to inhibit many of the types of behaviors that ADHD patients display in excess (Mattis, French, & Rapin, 1975).

Theoreticians, therefore, conclude that the reduction in metabolic activity measured on the PET scan must represent some defect in the brain structure, less observable than a lesion, but nonetheless real (Chelune, 1986). This is what is meant when parents are told that their child's ADHD is caused by a chemical imbalance in their brain.

Problems with the Logic of PET Studies

The logic of PET studies has two problems.

First and most obvious, both school tasks and Nintendo are continuous performance tasks. So if ADHD is due to a metabolic reduction in the frontal areas of the child's brain during continuous performance tasks, why does this deficit not also influence Nintendo continuous performance?

Clearly, these metabolic differences are not what accounts for the attentional problems of the ADHD child.

The second problem is methodological — the statistics are misused.

The Misuse of Statistics: Correlational Inference

There is no doubt that the data described by researchers is accurate. The problem is the rather glib conclusions they draw from it.

Just because a brain difference is observed between ADHD children and "normals" does not mean that this difference is due to some inherent structural or chemical imbalance in their brains. Nor does it mean that these differences are causative of anything — including ADHD. These differences could just as easily be the result of ADHD, as opposed to the cause of ADHD.

These conclusions are based on correlational data rather than experimental manipulations. Drawing causal conclusions from correlative data is always suspect. To appreciate the nature of this trap, we need to take a short detour into some basic statistics. Fear not, this is going to be easy stuff.

Correlation studies can only assert that two variables are, to some degree, changing in concert with one another, which is different than causing one another. Often some third factor causes the change in both of the variables that have been observed to change together.

A funny example of this is an old research finding that shows a strong correlation in college couples. This correlation is between the boyfriend's hand size and the girlfriend's buttock's size. One could hardly assume causation between these factors.

Actually, the causative variable in this example is likely that couples tend to pair up in relatively similar sizes.

Bigger guys match up with bigger girls and visa versa. So it is mate size preference, not hand size, that causes this correlation.

Another example is a correlation between mid-August pavement temperature in New York City and the banana crop in Brazil. Obviously, pavement temperatures in New York City do not influence bananas, but both are affected by global weather.

By the same token, one cannot assume that some difference between glucose metabolism in the frontal lobes of ADHD children, as opposed to "normals," is caused by some physiological difference in the child's brain structure. As we will see below, these differences are as likely learned as physiological.

To establish causation, one must experimentally manipulate the variables one theorizes to be causative. Since the variable is manipulated at the whim of the experimenter, it is assumed not to be under the control of any causative variables, such as preference for mate size or global weather.

By observing how the "caused" variable changes in response to the independent variable, which is impulsively tweaked by the experimenter, one can statistically establish the probability that there is a causal relationship between the two variables.

Let us take the example of an adolescent. If your son is not taking out the trash, but you want him to, you could likely get him to do it by paying him a dollar each time he takes it out. However, it might not be the dollar that makes him take out the trash. It may be that taking out the trash gives him an opportunity to surreptitiously smoke a cigarette in the back yard.

To find out, you could run an experiment to see if the dollar is what really causes him to take out the trash. First, you would pay him the dollar to take out the trash for a week. At that point, you do not know if it's the dollar that is motivating him to take out the trash.

To test this, you could stop giving him the dollar. If he stops taking out the trash, it is a good bet that the dollar motivated him. However, if he keeps taking out the trash, then something else is likely motivating him, such as sneaking a smoke.

If you have any doubt, you could alternate paying the dollar and not paying it to see how his trash-taking behavior changes in response to the payment. Only in this way can you be sure what factors are truly responsible for the observed changes.

The only meaningful way to determine the true cause of the measured differences between glucose metabolism of ADHD and normal children is to manipulate the theoretically causative variable — glucose metabolism — and see if ADHD behavior changes at the same time.

Preferably, these manipulations would be within a properly controlled experiment. Technically, we do not yet have the ability to do this. Until then, we will have to be satisfied with correlational statistics. And by the same token, we will have to limit our conclusions to statements about the co-occurrence of reduced glucose metabolism and ADHD, not the causal relationship between them.

Without jumping to conclusions, one can explore other plausible hypotheses to explain the data.

What About Learned Physiological Differences in Neurochemistry?

Correlational data are particularly vulnerable to alternate explanations, but let me offer you my preferred, alternate explanation. I prefer it because it helps explain how Computer Aided Emotional Restructuring (CAER) can so effectively treat ADHD children.

The Science

The brain is an electrochemical computer. Every thought, feeling, and movement is represented by an electrochemical state in the brain. The brain is chemically very malleable. It learns and stores information through subtle alterations in its chemistry and structure. These changes are not hypothetical or mysterious, but they are observable in a variety of ways.

One of the more common PET studies is to assess what part of the brain is used to think about particular things. Such studies measure changes in brain glucose metabolism, which are related to those thoughts. That is, they measure temporary physical changes in the brain due to temporary mental states. The subject thinks about something or performs some mental task while the PET data are being recorded.

In the case of the ADHD child, measurements are taken while he does continuous performance tasks, since these are similar to school tasks.

These temporary physical changes are the beginning of the learning process because, through the repetition of these temporary states, over time, the brain learns. And that happens because, as these temporary states are repeated, their corresponding neurochemical states become more permanent, i.e. they are learned.

Thus, the only way learning could be long lasting is if their corresponding neurochemical changes were also long lasting. It should be no surprise that these learned neurochemical changes are measurable as reduced glucose metabolism in the brains of ADHD children.

Just as easily, a PET researcher could ask the question: what emotional states have been conditioned in the ADHD patient by continuous performance tasks and how are they represented physiologically?

Clearly, it is not possible to PROVE either hypothesis with currently available data, but clinical experience tends to support the theory that ADHD is learned rather than the result of a defective brain.

Clinical Experience

Though current scientific literature provides no clues as to whether the differences in brain metabolism are structural or learned, my clinical experience points in the direction of the latter for two reasons.

First, though CAER treatment is powerful, it is unlikely to cause any lasting chemical or structural brain changes, other than changing learned states that are physiologically observable. My repeated success with ADHD patients must, therefore, be due to some change in their learning patterns.

Second, there are obvious chronic emotional states conditioned to school-related stimuli such as anxiety, anger, fear, embarrassment, and depression. ADHD children are very clear about this in their descriptions of school during CAER treatment.

They typically begin by talking about their boredom with school. When they explore this in CAER therapy, conjuring up images of teachers, specific academic subjects, tests, peers, and school itself, they express their feelings in vivid descriptions of frustration, anxiety, anger, nausea, and embarrassment.

The depth of feeling can be intense. For example, the CAER machine includes an anger bar, a two-inch wooden diameter bar that swings into bench press position. The anger bar allows patients to physically express their anger by pushing the bar while watching the CAER lights and thinking about what makes them angry. (Remember CAER treatment utilizes lights and sound.) This helps them fully experience their anger.

Trent, a 10-year-old ADHD boy, became so angry at his friends, teacher and older brother that he literally ripped the anger bar out of the CAER machine and broke it. Trent was not a malicious child. In fact, he was extremely apologetic about the damage to the bar.

These are precisely the noxious emotional experiences that the ADHD child seeks to avoid by applying strategies based on the Conditioned Attentional Avoidance

Loop Model. This is what one would expect if ADHD were learned attentional avoidance. When these emotions are extinguished with CAER, ADHD symptoms disappear. In the case of Trent, with CAER treatment, his anger subsided, which greatly improved his school performance.

ADHD Testing: Descriptive vs. Diagnostic

Another approach to making ADHD appear to be a well defined disorder is through tests given the child, his parents, and teachers. By attempting to capture convergent descriptions of ADHD, an illusion is generated that something of the essence of ADHD is being sorted out. This fascination with generated numbers approaches the mysticism of numerology.

The numbers are believed to divine some mystical wisdom about the child's inner cosmos. If these secrets are revealed, then we understand and it will be fixed. Let us now look at what we can really understand from these tests.

Differential diagnosis testing and descriptive testing are not the same thing.

Differential diagnosis testing is like taking a blood test to see whether you have a certain disease. With physical medicine, it is hoped that this diagnosis will allow the doctor to select just the right medicine that will then fix the problem.

Descriptive testing is designed to provide a fuller picture of the patterns and process demonstrated by the patient. This gives the doctor a broader information base to plan treatment. This type of testing seldom offers much new in terms of a definitive diagnosis, nor is it expected to.

Most psychological and educational testing is not differential diagnosis testing but, rather, descriptive testing. Many parents find this disappointing.

For example, many parents call my office asking if I do ADHD testing. The simple answer is no, but knowing that their stated question is not their real question, I try to give a more useful response.

Their real question is whether I can figure out what is wrong with their child and if I can fix it. To this question, I can usually answer yes.

Parents' distress is often most apparent over the phone as they tell the story they have told so many times. In rushed and desperate tones, Carol tells about her 11-year-old son, whose teacher declares he has ADHD, should be tested for ADHD, and should be put on Ritalin. He is failing most of his classes and is in trouble in the classroom.

Carol then goes on about her stepchildren, her irritable bowel syndrome, and her husband's drinking. But, she wants testing for her alleged ADHD son and wants to know what I think of Ritalin.

Because it is her prime concern, I at first focus on her son's issues by asking some probing questions about how he makes friends, plays computer games, and minds each parent.

From her answers to these questions, I can often begin, over the phone, to reframe the son's behavior — he has learned to adapt to the stresses in his family and school rather than having a neurological deficit.

This often relieves the parent and offers hope of being able to cure rather than control ADHD with medications.

Asking for ADHD testing is usually a plea for a diagnosis that someone knows what to do about. Parents are seeking help, and wanting their child tested for ADHD, in the same way they might want to find out if his symptoms are strep throat.

Implicitly, they assume that a psychological "Penicillin" might then be administered to kill the ADHD "bug." As of today, tests do not come close to providing this level of ADHD diagnostic power, nor is there any ADHD "Penicillin."

Even if learning disabilities and neuropsychological tests could identify the specific mental function that does not operate well, that would not mean that the function cannot function properly.

Tests only tap the state of the function during the testing procedure. Many factors effect cognitive and behavioral functioning, particularly the child's emotional response to the testing procedure.

Only to the extent that the testing situation is similar to school will responses parallel those obtained in school. But no testing procedures come with 29 other kids, the textbooks the child hates, and the child next to him who laughs at him.

Since the testing situation is usually very dissimilar to the attentionally avoided classroom stimuli, the test is not measuring what teachers and parents are seeing as ADHD.

This is not to say that assessment instruments are worthless. Behavior checklists can be useful tools for clinical or research purposes, but they are not useful to capture the presence of an underlying pathology such as ADHD.

Even if you assume that these tests measure some deep learning or neurological process, it does not mean that they refer to any neurological deficit. From the framework of the Conditioned Attentional Avoidance Loop Model, it is apparent that these tests are just identifying the specific link in the learning or performance chain that has been inhibited by the attentional avoidance, anxiety, or depression.

Inhibition does not act mysteriously. It has a direct, definable, observable effect, and that is what educational and psychological tests are measuring, nothing more. Statements about neurological deficits based on these tests are pure speculation.

That means that there are other quite plausible explanations for the same data. For example, the attentional, memory and understanding mechanisms may be potentially fully functional but inhibited for some reason by anxiety (Logan & Cowan 1984). We have all had experiences in which we became so anxious that we forgot certain learning or performance skills.

Many of us have stood in front of a group of people to give a speech and, although we have practiced for hours, we have forgotten what we intended to say. Blanking out on an exam is a comparable experience of anxiety-inhibiting performance. The Conditioned Attentional Avoidance Loop Model postulates that a similar emotional inhibition of learning and performance is a component of ADHD.

The Bottom-line on the Clinical Relevance of ADHD Testing

To illustrate the relevance of ADHD testing in a clinical setting, an example from my personal experience might help.

I used to like to chide my orthopedist. I would hurt my knee, so I would lay off of it for a few weeks. If it didn't get better, I would visit my orthopedist and tell him, "Doc, I hurt my knee climbing last month. It hurts when I do like this or that. I have been laying off of it for a few weeks to let it recover. Would you take a look at it and see what you think."

After some poking and bending it, an X-ray, and an MRI, my orthopedist typically would come back and say, "Looks like you hurt your knee. It will probably hurt when you bend it this way or that. Probably better lay off of it for a while."

Somehow it sounds like I ended up right back where I started. And so it is with psychological testing of ADHD children. Parents bring their child to the psychologist and say, "Doc, my kid can't do one thing for long, particularly in the classroom. His grades are terrible. He doesn't have many friends. He won't mind. You know, he sure likes his Nintendo. He can do that for hours without a break."

The child is given a series of tests; teachers and parents are given questionnaires. All this is fed into a computer to make it seem more scientific. Out pours the report.

The psychologist then tells the parents, "Looks like Josh has a pretty good case of ADHD."

Mom and dad ask, "What does that mean?"

The Psychologist answers, "He probably can't do one thing for long, particularly in the classroom. His grades are likely to be terrible. He probably doesn't have many friends and doesn't mind very well. But you know these kids can usually play Nintendo for hours without a break."

These types of expensive reports regularly come with ADHD children who are referred to me. In looking over my files of these rather impressive documents (and they really are impressive), a pattern appears. There is a wide range of truly insightful measurements, descriptions, and analyses of children and their problems, but the recommended treatments are sadly narrow and redundant.

This is not an indictment of my peers' professional prowess; it is rather a factual representation of the narrow range of treatment options we now possess. There are more options for generating reports than treatments.

Today, there are only four or five different treatment options available for ADHD children — behavior therapy medications, tutoring, family therapy and now Computer Aided Emotional Restructuring (CAER).

Frequently a therapist will use most of these options.

Behavior therapy is easy and generally helpful.

I seldom recommend medications because most of the children who come to me are already on them. The medications are obviously not working. If they were, the children would not have been referred to me. Since I consider medications a rare last resort, most of my calls to the child's physician are to recommend a reduction in medications.

Tutoring is usually an option late in therapy if the child has fallen behind academically — so much so that he is having a hard time catching up, even after the emotional and attentional problems have been resolved.

CAER is usually my treatment of choice because it produces faster results for a broader range of children and parents. The emphasis of CAER is on treatment, not testing. And the information needed to guide the process is gleaned from conversations with the child and family.

This is why I very rarely do any testing.

Anxious to Diagnose ADHD ... "We've Got to Do Something About This"

For me, one of the scariest human proclivities is the pressure to act even when we have no idea what the effective action may be, or even what the consequences of the action may be. To the actor, action in itself is satisfying, regardless of the consequence of the action.

One of the major forces driving the popularity of the ADHD diagnosis is the clear relationship between diagnosis and treatment. The ADHD diagnosis serves as license to act, to do "something," and has a particularly powerful meaning in the school and medical system.

The ADHD diagnosis represents the immediate authority to put the child on stimulant medications. In other words, generally, ADHD equals Ritalin. And if the child is lucky, a little behavior modification is thrown in.

This neat "diagnosis = treatment" equation is very rare in the behavioral sciences.

But parents and teachers feel a sense of helplessness and frustration with ADHD children, so the Ritalin mandate is tantalizing.

This in itself is not bad. The literature is clear. Ritalin is helpful in the short run for many of these children, but the problem is much more complex than giving a child a pill. In fact, if the solution to ADHD were as simple as taking a pill, these children would not show up in my office in large numbers. But they do. And in my clinical experience, Ritalin does seem to be quite helpful in the short term, but in a year or two it is no longer very beneficial.

Opposition to the Ritalin Mandate

There is growing concern, if not outrage, about this Ritalin mandate. The cover story on the March 18, 1996 Newsweek was entitled "Ritalin" by LynNell Hancock. The idea of giving large numbers of children "speed" on a regular basis is arousing public suspicion. The article reiterates many of the points I have made.

There is too much pressure to put children on Ritalin. "School psychologists ... say they feel pressed to recommend pills first before they have time to do an evaluation."

Dr. Peter Jensen, Chief of the Child and Adolescent Disorders Research Branch of NIMH, says,

> *"I fear that ADHD is suffering from the disease-of-the-month syndrome," in spite of the fact that it is generally agreed that "most children need behavior-modification therapy and special help in school. But most of the surveyed pediatricians say they rarely recommend anything more than pills. A lot of doctors ... are lulled into complacency. They think that by giving a child Ritalin, the likelihood of helping him is high and the downside is low."*

Not to overlook the vigilance of my own profession, a recent article in the APA Monitor (Feb. 1995) decries the overuse of the ADHD label, especially at the loss of delving into the individual child's unique configuration of issues.

There is consensus that the solution is more complex than just prescribing a pill.

Chapter 13

CAER: A New Treatment Technology

Computer Aided Emotional Restructuring is mostly a non-verbal therapy and departs from traditional therapy in two ways. First, it is more of a do-it-yourself therapy, as opposed to a therapist imparting his or her professional knowledge. Second, it is unlearning emotional patterns, i.e. destructive coping mechanisms, rather than learning new skills or knowledge.

CAER as Do-It-Yourself Therapy

In traditional psychological therapy, the patient is referred to a therapist whose job it is to sort out distressing thoughts until a problem is resolved. The patient translating his feelings and internal experience into words — words that are intended to convey information to the therapist, accomplishes this.

Then, after only an hour or two of a therapist gathering this thin word stream of information, he or she begins to subtly or directly shape the patient's thinking and behavior.

This traditional model of therapy has always seemed a bit presumptuous to me. Its flaw is that the words only convey a tiny fraction of information, especially when that information is compared to the vast knowledge and experience within the patient.

You — the patient — live inside your head all of your life. You are the world's expert on you. No one has one one-millionth of the information and experience you have within yourself — even if some of this information is a bit inaccurate or disorganized.

Given the right situation and guidance, it would seem that the patient, with his vastly greater and more in-depth understanding of himself, is in a much better position to direct the therapeutic process.

CAER is able to access this vast store of self-knowledge without having to reduce it to words and, therefore, is much more efficient than traditional talk therapy.

Unlearning Emotional Patterns vs. Learning New Skills and Knowledge

CAER's other difference from traditional therapy is equally important. Traditional therapy is predicated on two assumptions:

1) The expression of feelings provides catharsis.
2) The problems that bring the patient to therapy are a function of a lack of some knowledge or skill.

In other words, patients are simply bottling up their feelings or they don't understand how to do whatever it is that will solve their problems.

The task of the psychotherapy patient is to learn the knowledge and skills necessary to express feelings, to express those feelings, AND to change behaviors to prevent further buildup of negative feelings. The therapist's task is to teach the skills. It is a student-teacher relationship.

But this is incongruent with my observations about patients, both children and adults. Almost all of my patients have at some time demonstrated all the skills they need. In fact, they demonstrate them in other situations, but not in the problem situation — be it school, home, marriage or the work place.

They may be a successful manager at work — communicating, asserting, disciplining, and listening all day long. These are most likely the same skills they need for parenting or being an effective spouse.

In the case of ADHD children, successful skills are clearly present in some instances. For example, they often interact well in one-to-one situations such as with an adult or with a favorite friend. However in the problem situation, most often the classroom or the home, these skills seem to fly out the window.

Emotional Inhibition of Skills

Why is it the ADHD child is skillful in some areas but not in others?

It seems unlikely that he magically forgets skills in the classroom or when doing homework but remembers them when playing with a friend or Nintendo. The most likely reason is that the child is inhibited by emotions triggered by the problem situation.

ADHD children have learned to respond to the problem situation with anxiety, anger, fear, or depression. This causes two things to happen.

First, the increased emotional arousal overwhelms access to the skills required to cope with the situation. Second, these feelings trigger the Conditioned Attentional Avoidance Loop so that the child is mentally absent from the situation.

Traditional therapy attempts to teach the ADHD child coping skills to the problem areas in his life, tools that are already at his disposal.

This is like teaching someone to ride a bicycle on north-south streets when they regularly ride only on east-west streets. If they do not ride on north-south streets, it seems very unlikely that it is because of some lack of skills or knowledge.

More likely, there is some barrier to riding on north-south streets, such as fear possibly resulting from crashing on a north-south street. As absurd as this sounds, continuing to train previously demonstrated skills is what most educational and psychological therapy emphasizes.

Rather than teaching skills that are already demonstrated by the child, it would seem cleverer to remove the emotional obstacles that are in the problem situation. Eliminating fear of north-south streets is more effective than giving bicycle-riding lessons. This is exactly the contrast between CAER and the more skills training orientation of traditional ADHD therapy.

Sara: A Parent's Experience With CAER

Sara was a manager in an aerospace company. She was responsible for more than 40 employees. All day long she listened to their problems, solved conflicts, gave directives, reinforced positive performance and disciplined problem behaviors. It was apparent that she did this well — she received outstanding performance evaluations and had moved up in the company very quickly.

Although she could maintain her highly effective behavior at work, her behavior at home was very different. In the half hour drive from work to home, she became "stressed out, angry and frustrated." By the time she walked through the door at home, she was a different person. She was no longer the competent people manager. She was a yelling, angry, frustrated parent who was contributing to her son's ADHD.

Sara said she could feel the change coming over her as she drove closer to her home. At work, she felt competent and in charge. At home, she felt overwhelmed, depressed and helpless. At home, she was not able to do the very same behaviors that worked so well for her at work.

There seemed very little reason to teach her the skills she ably demonstrated at work. Besides, she read many parenting, ADHD, and behavior modification books. She had the tools, she just couldn't do them at home.

To remedy the problem, we focused her CAER treatment on extinguishing the "stressed out, angry, frustrated, depressed and helplessness" that she experienced at home. In two sessions, it became apparent that some of those feelings were the result of a troubled marriage, which we then addressed.

After two sessions, she had few of those negative feelings at home, and she was able to be as competent a parent as she was a manager.

CAER as a Tool for Change

Explaining the Conditioned Attentional Avoidance Loop Model to a child, teacher, parents, or researcher is unlikely to be of any help unless it leads to a tool for change and eradicating the symptoms of ADHD. The Conditioned Attentional Avoidance Loop Model does, though, provide us with a useful blueprint for creating the tools for emotional change. And CAER is that engine of intervention in the equation of change.

Chapter 14

The Viewpoint From all Corners

Seeing With a Different Eye

In the last fifty years, biochemistry and medicine have made enormous, beneficial gains in the understanding of many human maladies. These successes have strongly reinforced our tendency toward physical explanations of our problems.

In many ways this has worked well, but there is a rising crop of "disorders" that do not seem to respond well to this strategy. Included in this list are ADHD, learning disabilities, behavior disabilities, asthma, allergies, rheumatoid arthritis, lupus, chronic fatigue syndrome, irritable bowel syndrome, fibromyalgia, and chronic pain syndrome (Bellavite & Signorini, 1995.) Also, the pursuit of solutions on a molecular level has obscured the fact that humans are the most powerful learning machines on the planet.

We think of the nervous system as the primary learning system, but that is only one aspect of our learning

ability.   The immune system is at least as powerful a
learning mechanism. We also learn all the way down to the
cellular level (Dworkin, 1994). If we do not address these
powerful learning effects, we will not effectively treat many
of the chronic illnesses or ADHD.

One of my personal gurus was Fritz Perls, the
developer of Gestalt Therapy. Gestalt Therapy places great
emphasis on seeing and acting on the obvious. When asked
about how he did his therapeutic wizardry, Perls would
answer, "All I do is make the implicit explicit and state the
obvious." His magic was based on very careful observation
of what was directly under his nose.   In a world of
meditating on hidden psychological obscurities, his ability
to respond to the obvious seemed magical.

Looking at the Child, Rather than the Label

Whenever a new family with a troubled child comes
to me for help, there is pressure from the school and
parents to decide whether he has ADHD. I prefer to duck
this issue and avoid lending my professional authority to
this label. I want to see the child as he is.

I want the parents to do likewise. Since my office is
often the court of last resort, it is sometimes difficult to
separate the child from all the labels prior helpers have
pinned on him.   Parents and teachers tell me he is
immature, dyslexic, ADHD, has learning disabilities,
behavior disabilities, Tourette's syndrome, impulse control
problems, is aggressive, auditory, depressed, co-depen-
dent, etc., etc., etc.

By the time he appears in my office, he has become
these labels. I guess I am not too swift, but these terms do
not conjure up imagery of the child that is of any use. To be
helpful, I need mental pictures about concrete events that
occur in specific situations, such as home or school. I am
looking for the exact stimuli that set off the problem and the
reinforcers that maintain it.

My approach is straightforward as I search for firm examples of the problem. Can he stay in his seat during math class? What makes his inattention better or worse? Does he raise his hand before speaking in class? What happens if he speaks out of turn in class? Does he play cooperatively with other children? Do they seem to like him? How and where does he do his homework? Who, if anyone, supervises homework and how? Does he like computer games? What do you say or do that upsets him? What have you tried before and with what results?

In order not to obscure the child with this professional mumbo jumbo, I have to get back to basic behavioral observations. Many times I resort to asking, "What would I see if I were the mouse in the corner? What would I see when...?" Not only am I trying to find out how he functions but also, what function his behavior is serving.

What Parents Say

The emotional outpouring from parents of ADHD children is usually overwhelming. In fact, their emotions are as powerful as the child's. When describing their children, the parents lapse in to descriptions of their own feelings of irritation, anger, frustration, helplessness, depression, anxiety, embarrassment, and shame. They use phrases like:

"He drives me nuts."
"I feel so helpless."
"I can't stand it when...."
"I can never do anything without him..."
"I really don't like him."

These intense emotions are an important part of ADHD because they are reinforcers and punishers. They are reinforcers and punishers not carried simply in the words used, but also in the parents' tones of voice and speech rhythms.

Alice told me about her son, "Bengie drives me crazy when he fights with his older sister." "I am really uptight when the phone rings," she said, "because I am always afraid it's the school calling to tell me what he has done this time. Lately, I've started having headaches, and I'm irritable and tired all the time."

Alice and her husband were fighting over how to handle Bengie. Her husband wanted to get tougher with Bengie to make him "tow the line", but she thought Bengie was already under too much stress. And she felt guilty about making his life even more miserable.

Their fighting about Bengie began to erode their marriage. Alice had begun taking Prozac. It didn't seem to be adequate.

Parents are active agents in the creation and cure of ADHD.

The Child's Experience

Though younger children feel the same aversion to school work as older children, they are more hesitant to express their aversion because of their dependency on adults. Seven-year-old Jacob felt that his friend Jeb "won't let me play any more. He hits me."

When Jacob talked about his teacher, he described her as "mean and she yells at me." When asked why she yells, he replied, "She doesn't like me. She's mean." He would also say, "I don't like reading. It makes me mad."

You could hear not only anger, but also fear, in his voice.

Early school children often have a hard time figuring out what is going wrong. They just know it feels bad.

What Teachers Say

Teachers' professionalism does not protect them from exhibiting the same emotional involvement as parents. They say things like:

"He exhausts me."
"I feel like strangling him sometimes."
"I'm glad I have only three more years to retirement."
"I feel sorry for young teachers starting out, having to spend their career with children like we're seeing now."

Though it's easy to sympathize, their language is descriptive of the interlocking dynamics between adult and child. It's just that their exposure to a particular ADHD child is limited. They spend part of each day, Monday through Friday for one year, with the child. So, their learning history is not as intense as the parents'.

But words and phrases, such as short attention span, aggressive, repeat offender, and immature, are often used to express in professional terms the same feelings parents have.

Yet, we unrealistically expect professionals to be objective and unemotional, even if the kid slugs them. Children are expert at reading the subtle signals of the underlying emotional arousal, whether verbal or nonverbal.

This response is exactly parallel to the ADHD child's loss of focus on his schoolwork and his emotionally driven attentional avoidance. The only difference is that the child, feeling powerless, resorts to attentional avoidance rather than pouring out his feelings.

What we are describing here are two sides of the very same ADHD coin. On the one hand, we have conditioned outrage by the adults and, the other, the child's attentional avoidance. Neither could exist without the other because each provides the reinforcement for the other.

This is not meant as criticism of the adults, but rather as a description of the natural unfolding of both sides of the dynamics of the ADHD situation.

What Teachers Don't See

One of the comments that I have gotten from some teachers who have read early drafts of this book is "We do not do that," "We are not negative to the child," "We reward not punish the child."

When you are on the power side of a conflict, it is easy not to see what you are doing. The typical white person has a difficult time understanding why a person of color cannot feel, think and act like a white.

We live in a culture that believes in the myth that what we get is a direct result of our personal merit, be it hard work, intelligence, moral virtue, athletic skills or beauty. Because of this, whites often see the person of color as causing his own problems by not working hard enough.

The ADHD child is in the same position. He is often treated as if his problem is the result of not working hard enough, or as more commonly stated, screwing around.

Therefore, the ADHD label, with all of its medical trappings, is as pejorative as "nigger." These negative messages do their damage whether directed at people of color or the ADHD child.

And just as with people of color, you cannot understand the discrimination by talking to the power side of the conflict. You have to listen to him, a person of color.

Likewise, to understand the predicament of the ADHD child, you have to listen to him, not the teacher who holds power over him. When you do talk to the child, the anger, anxiety, fear, and guilt he feels in response to school is unmistakable.

This is not to say that teachers, any more than most whites, intend to demean those they have power over. In fact, it is difficult to do something intentionally that you are not aware of. That's why, part of the thrust of this book, is to see ADHD through the experience of the child.

It is important because:

1) Only through the ADHD child's eyes can you understand what turns him on and off, attentionally, academically, and behaviorally.

2) To secure the child's participation, you have to solve the problem as he defines it. And the child always has a view of the problem. Many times it is quite different from how adults define it.

3) You have to understand the child's point of view to have a self-sustaining cure for ADHD — because the cure has to work for him.

4) It is the ADHD child's experience of his world, not ours, that drives his behavior.

5) Not to understand the ADHD child's experience of his world is to offer him solutions to our problems with him, rather than solutions to his problem.

Only in this way, can we understand why the ADHD child cannot stop screwing around, work harder and be like other kids. The cost of this approach may be to alienate those in power, such as teachers, counselors and school administrators. Not to take the risk, though, is to perpetuate the blindness that has contributed to ADHD.

What Children Say

The children themselves are the most interesting participants to listen to. ADHD children are quite clear about what the problem is, if you listen.

If you listen, they tell you clearly about their daily classroom experiences. They are mad at their peers, frustrated with their school, anxious about their poor performance, and mad at their teacher. They express extreme embarrassment, depression, and helplessness. These aversive feelings are what drive ADHD.

As the Teacher Sees It

As the Child Sees It

ADHD Children are Not Pathological Liars

Jeff was a macho 13-year-old who tried to wear the image that he had everything that counted, together. He told me he had many friends and gave me the names of his many friends. According to him, he was also doing "good" in school.

His mother told me that "good" meant he was only getting four F's and two D's this quarter, rather than his usual six F's. For him, it was an improvement, but it was nothing to brag about. His mother went on to tell me that Jeff was in constant conflict with his few friends. He tended to boss them around and play very rough, which eventually distanced him from most children.

When I talked to Jeff's teacher, I heard the same story. His disruptive, outspoken manner in class earned him an outcast status among the other children. They laughed at his antics in class, but they wanted little to do with him on the playground. Yet, his macho performances did seem to earn him some fearful respect from his male peers.

When Jeff and I discussed what his mother and teacher had told me, he, at first, responded with defensive confusion, restating, "I got lotsa friends. We hang out together at the mall and do things."

For him, there was no contradiction. He defined anyone of his age who shared the mall with him as a friend. He had developed a personal meaning of friend that really was not in conflict with what many adolescent males do in malls. Sometimes, there is little interaction between them. They simply stand quietly in groups, with little conversation, hanging out. So, Jeff did not stand as close to the others. For him, that was not significant.

As to the grades, he was right, in a sense. As he said, "I'm doing better than I was last semester, aren't I?" He was doing well relative to his historical performance. He was looking at his personal best, which it was.

Is not personal best an acceptable standard for amateur athletes?

He was no more a liar than the amateur Bloomsday runner who says he did well this year with a time of one hour, fifty-two minutes — when the professional runners were finishing in 34 minutes. But it was good race for the amateur; it was the first time he had broken two hours.

So, is he lying when he says, "Did good this year"? If he is, there are many middle-aged, well-respected doctors, lawyers, judges, accountants, and psychologists who tell big lies every May in Spokane, Washington after running in the Bloomsday Race.

ADHD children are a bundle of emotional contradictions. There is a big difference in how they present themselves on the surface versus underneath the surface, or from one situation to another. Their explicitly expressed state is usually more positive than what impartial observation supports. Let us look at some of these contrasts.

In spite of poor peer relationships and poor school performance, ADHD kids regularly report that they are doing well in school, have many friends, and get along at home. In fact, the opposite is usually true.

However, from their conscious perspective, what they say is likely true. I certainly do not think they are pathological liars. Rather, the ADHD child's attentional avoidance serves as a filter. Subtle, negative, emotional precursors serve as cues that trigger attentional avoidance before negative experience reaches consciousness.

Negative experience is selectively filtered out and only the positive is allowed through to the conscious level. For example, despite rejection by their peers, they will typically say that they have many friends. What happens in this example is that when interactions with peers become negative, the ADHD child "checks out" by attentionally avoiding. Thus, he does not experience the negative input at the conscious level.

Though negative feedback does not reach conscious awareness, it is processed at a subconscious level. The constant intake of this negative feedback at a subconscious level causes the depression so often found in ADHD children.

Carefully Watch the Obvious

In the traditions of Gestalt Therapy and Behavior Analysis, we can learn much by careful observation, including listening to the ADHD child and those in his world. What is under your nose is often what is really going on.

Jeff and Kent, Two ADHD Boys

Interviewing these well-trained evaders is like trying to grab a wet bar of soap in the shower. Jeff was a typical case.

> I asked, "How are you doing in school?"
> He answered, "Good."
> I asked, "How do you get along with your parents?"
> He answered, "Pretty good."
> "What do you like to do?"
> "Hang around."

Because of these defense strategies, I now try to avoid approaching children this way. Instead, I start off with both the child and the parents in the room. I ask the parents what brings them to see me. Typically, like Jeff's parents, they go on about all the things their son is doing wrong.

"He fights. He's failing school. He doesn't pay attention. He kicks the dog."

I listen attentively, but I don't side with them too strongly. I do not engage the child much. He is just listening to his parents' story. I do watch him, though, to see what feelings his parents' report triggers in him.

After the parents tell their story, I ask them to sit in the waiting room so that I can talk to their son in private. After they leave, I comment, in kid language, on the feelings the parents triggered in him. I say, "It really makes you mad when they say that stuff, doesn't it? Or, "It really ticks you off when they say that stuff about you."

If I can't read the child well, I will say something more general like, "Okay, now what is the rest of the story."

I am always very careful not to side with the child against the parents. Since I am tapping into the child's feelings and learning history relative to these issues, he usually just pours out his frustrations. This not only helps me gain rapport with him, but I also get to see the world through his eyes. I can then begin to build an alliance to help him solve his problems as he defines them.

Amazingly, this also solves most of the problems his parents enumerated. The child is just as unhappy about his situation as his parents are. He just talks about it differently and puts a different emphasis on the issues.

In an interview with 15-year-old Kent, I did precisely what I described. As is usual with most such kids, he poured out his resentments. "They never get off my back, no matter what I do. They won't believe me that I am doing better in school. They just keep ragging on me. Who cares? I'm leaving home the day I turn 18."

Kent was frustrated that his parents did not respond positively to his smallest efforts. And when they didn't, he sank deeper into a greater sense of helplessness. He continued to complain about parents, peers, teachers and school work for the rest of the hour.

His parents were amazed he was talking to me. In my initial phone conversation, they had said, "He probably won't talk. The last counselor he had couldn't get a word out of him."

Chapter 15

Stimulants vs. Conditioned Attentional Avoidance

Josh, an 11-Year-Old ADHD Boy

Josh, an 11-year-old, had a long history of unsuccessful ADHD treatment in England and the U.S. — five years worth when he was brought to me for treatment. Despite his initial medication of 20 mg spansual (time release) of Ritalin in the morning and a 10 mg tablet at noon, his behavior was very disruptive both at home and school.

His angry outbursts were directed at peers, teachers, siblings, and parents. In fact, during the third week of treatment, when his teacher touched him, he wheeled around so violently that he sprained her wrist.

Josh also reported that his little seven-year-old brother, as well as many of his peers, made him mad. But unlike many ADHD kids, Josh was well liked by his peers, though he did not like many of them.

Josh's mother was the dominant figure in the family. His father clearly had ADHD/R, and the school expressed concern that his younger brother was also showing signs of

ADHD. But his parents were very compliant with all requests.

In the initial session, his parents were given a five-minute cassette to record the statements they made that provoked their son. At the same session, Josh was simply asked to "think about things that bug you, like kids at school, your teacher, your parents and your little brother." He was told to get as mad as he could at them. These thoughts initially provoked substantial anger.

At the second session, the parents were given a second five-minute cassette and asked to have the teacher record all the things she said that provoked him. Also, at that session, Josh's parents' tape was played to him. Over the next several sessions, the anger provoked by both the tape and the general instruction to get mad abated.

By the fourth session, his parents were reporting some improvement at home, but Josh's classroom behavior was still a major problem.

Due to resistance by the school, we received only an incomplete tape in the fifth week of treatment. At that time, I doubted the effectiveness of the procedure and sent the cassette back to the teacher for completion. An attempt was made to use the partial cassette to desensitize Josh. He, however, was unable to focus because of the poor quality of the tape.

It turned out, though, that this was a major juncture for his school behavior. Josh has had NO significant school problems since that session.

By the sixth session, little emotional response could be evoked in him. The sixth and seventh sessions were used to completely eliminate past problem behaviors at home and school and to prepare Josh for a reduction in Ritalin.

Also, in that seventh week, a usable tape was forwarded from Josh's school. It was played to him several times just to make sure that the desensitization really had been complete. It was. At the seventh session, the pediatrician gave permission to begin to slowly reduce Josh's medications.

The Ritalin had clearly developed some superstitious value. Josh's mother was anxious about the idea of reducing it, though she could articulate no rationale for it except, "just in case."

Several more sessions were spent, mostly to reassure the parents, while slowly stepping Josh off the medications. No regression of his behavior occurred during this process. He continues to function well without medication.

His father was also successfully treated for ADHD/R using CAER.

The Attentional Function of Stimulant Drugs

ADHD children may go from task to task with little visible continuity. They appear scattered, impulsive, and, if they have suffered much negative feedback, irritable and aggressive.

Their attentional breaks make their behavior seem disjointed and non-purposive. This disjointedness comes from their attention alternately being under willful vs. conditioned control, i.e. from each master dictating a different direction.

Stimulant medications serve to increase the willful control of attention. With Ritalin, the ADHD child is able to willfully override the conditioned attentional avoidance patterns, which in turn enables him to more easily direct his attention to the tasks he wishes to do and those in his environment wish him to do.

The stimulant functions just as my espresso did in my personal example in the third chapter.

The Short Term Utility of Ritalin

Reviews of the literature on the use of Ritalin (Carlson, et. al., 1993) show that there is an acute, positive effect on daily classroom performance.

But studies of achievement over months or years fail to provide evidence of longer term, beneficial medication effects. My own clinical experience strongly supports this lack of long-term usefulness of stimulants.

Likely what is going on is that the learned attentional avoidance continues to strengthen and refine until it can overpower chemically enhanced willful attention, just as it once overpowered willful attention not enhanced by stimulants.

Therefore, enhancement of willful attention through stimulant drugs provides a tiny, often short-lived escape from this problem.

Mental Isometrics

The internal conflict between efforts toward avoidance versus efforts toward compliance places the child in a tug-of-war within himself.

First, we teach him to develop strong self-control skills in order to meet the behavioral demands of the classroom, such as sitting in the seat and working quietly. Then, we enhance his ability to do this by giving him Ritalin, but the classroom is still aversive to the child.

The tug-of-war that ensues as a result of stimulants fighting noxious input creates a form of mental isometrics, ADHD versus Ritalin. ADHD serves to help the child reduce his experience of the emotionally painful situation; Ritalin empowers him to maintain contact with it.

Attentional Tug –A – War

There is, though, another common approach to forcing attentional contact with the negative classroom experience — contingency management. Typically, contingency management means providing rewards for tolerating unpleasant school experiences, such as performing the school work.

This places the child in another battle within himself. His set of conditioned responses is trying to direct his attention away from the noxious stimuli, while another set is trying to direct the his attention toward it.

The dilemma we create for the ADHD child is the same as persuading an adult, with offers of money, to hold the palm of his hand over a candle until burned.

On one side, the learned motivational power of money would dictate forcing the hand over the candle. But on the other side, the reflexive, physiological reaction to pain would dictate withdrawal from the candle.

One way to deal with the pain of the flame would be to think about something else, which in essence is how most pain control strategies work, including ADHD. But this war between two opposing alternatives uses so much energy that nothing gets accomplished, except anxiety, tension, and mental exhaustion. Adults trapped in this situation develop ulcers, headaches, anxiety disorders, irritable bowel syndrome, and so on.

With the ADHD child, a more elegant, efficient, and less tension- and pain-producing strategy is to eliminate the child's learned aversive responses to schoolwork, homework, parents, teachers, peers and the classroom.

Learning situations are not inherently negative. Rather, the surrounding social experience turns it, over time, from neutral to negative.

This is similar to developing an acquired aversion to, say, the game of Scrabble. I, for one, hate Scrabble. It is not because of anything inherent in the nature of the game. Rather, it is because of my experience with it. I am a terrible Scrabble player. So, I always lose by miles. Losing sometimes is not bad, but losing all the time makes the game a depressing and aversive experience that I avoid.

Like any other learned response, it is possible to extinguish these learned aversive emotional responses. The idea of CAER treatment is to reduce, rather than oppose, the learned emotional forces that cause the child's attention to be diverted from school tasks. Once the mental isometrics are removed, setting internal forces in opposition does not waste energy, and mild forms of behavior therapy can then be very useful.

This is the same as putting out the candle. If the candle were not hot, it would take very little money to get an adult to place his hand above it.

So it is with the ADHD child and schoolwork.

The Exhausting Struggle

Chapter 16

Thinking Models and ADHD

A New Approach to Thinking Models We Use and Their Hidden Assumptions

Discussions about ADHD, its causes and cures, have a certain superficiality about them. We have grown accustomed to hidden meanings that are implicit but not fully understood, which has lead to some false conclusions and ineffective action. In order to correct these misunderstandings, we need to examine our biases and how they affect our attitudes and actions regarding ADHD.

However, if we are going to be able to think differently about ADHD, we first need to discuss these common thinking patterns and the limitations they impose.

The Mechanical vs. Learning Model of Human Thinking, Feeling, Behavior, and Physiology

The Mechanical Model

Like a cue ball hitting a pool ball, we cause each other's behavior. That is, one person transfers the motive force to another at the instant of interaction, just as when the cue ball hits the pool ball. This is thinking of human interaction in mechanical terms.

This mechanical model implies that the strength of the impact (signal, input action, words, etc.) directly relates to the speed of the second ball (the strength of the response, the yelling and disruption it elicits in the recipient).

One sees this in how adults explain interactions with children in bewildered terms. The adults will say things such as, "I only asked if his homework was done. But then he screamed, broke, and hit...." It is always some incredulously explosive response.

The adults are rightly puzzled as to how their question could have powered such outrage. But it didn't power it; it only released it. The response was already there, like a compressed spring, fully energized and ready to activate. The fact that the response was out of proportion to the stimulus is confusing, unless you consider the learning history of similar interactions.

The problem with the mechanical model is that it does not consider prior occurrences of similar processes, that is, the learning history. The mechanical model only implies that each incidence of stimulus and response are discrete and in proportion.

In other words, the mechanical model makes a poor explanation for human behavior at any level, all the way down to the biochemical level.

If it is so poor, why do we avidly stick to it?

We stick to it because the mechanical model is much more intuitive than the idea that we learn over time. The mechanical model is an extension of our domain-specific understanding of the physical world. Domain-specific learning is the idea that we are born with the basic framework for understanding the world already built into our minds.

The most obvious example of domain-specific learning is language. We are born with the ability to make all the necessary sounds for all human languages. We also have a basic language structure and syntax with which we organize these sounds into language. Similar inherent information and organizing mechanisms have been identified for a large range of human capabilities (Hirshfield & Gelman, 1994).

Another example of domain-specific learning is our inherent understanding of how basic physical objects interact. We use this to know how hard to throw a ball, how to position a lever or the amount of liquid we can pour from one container to another.

That we are born with a basic intuitive understanding of the physical properties of the world around us does not mean that our understanding is always accurate. Intuitive and accurate are not necessarily the same thing. There are well-documented inaccuracies in our folk physics, as our domain-specific understandings are technically termed (Hirshfield & Gelman, 1994).

For instance, contrary to our intuitive belief, the laws of physics indicate that a body in motion will continue in motion, without assistance, until it is acted on by another force. In our common experience, this other force is usually friction, wind resistance, or an opposing force. Nevertheless, our intuitive view is contradictory to the laws of physics.

Every study of naive physics conceptions reports some variant of a belief that, if an object is in motion, there must be a force acting on the object.   This belief fits naturally with the presumption that motion requires explanation, together with the assumption that an explanation must specify a causal agent ... external agent pushes, pulls, shoves and all kinds of direct mechanical actions of one body on another.... Virtually all naive thinkers about motion express the belief that objects will slow down and eventually stop if force is not applied externally ... (which is) a special case of a "dying away" primitive (pattern) that expresses the belief that all events naturally come to an end. (Resnick, 1994)

Will Rogers, the famous humorist, summed it up well. He said, "Most of what we know just ain't so."

Even though we tend to equate intuitive with true, "it just ain't so." Generalizing the action of physical objects to the action of people on other people, as one social object to another, is also inaccurate. This amounts to extending "folk physics" beyond physical bodies and on to social bodies. When the results of this translation do not conform to our "folk physics" predictions, we are bewildered.

The learning model adds the dimension of time and experience to the mechanical model to provide a more accurate explanation of social interactions, particularly the behavior of ADHD children.

The Learning Model

In a sense, learning connects all of us to our environment, just like the strings on a puppet connect to the puppeteer.

These learned threads automatically trigger our corresponding behavior. When someone walks up and sticks out his hand, it is almost impossible not to automatically reach for that hand and shake it — as though an invisible puppeteer pulled a hand string.

Most of these automatic responses serve us very well to simplify our lives. Such automatic responses, though, are learned slowly, over time, with repetition and reinforcement. Just telling someone he should reciprocate with a reached out hand when another person initiates a similar action seldom works well. Sometimes he will remember. But many times, in complicated and emotionally loaded situations, he will forget.

In those situations, learning history pulls other puppet strings, instead of remembering to put a hand forward.

This is precisely the problem with instructing parents and teachers and children in behavior modification. Though instruction will help in calm, low stress situations, it will seldom have much effect in the heat of battle.

Thus, the key variable in the learning model is learning through experience over an extended period of time.

For the ADHD child, such learning imbues individual words, people, books, and classrooms with powerful emotional meanings, as well as a power over the ADHD child that is not apparent to adults.

When the adult requests something from the child, the strength of the adult's words is less important than the learned negative emotional responses it triggers in the child.

The ADHD child just has to be able to perceive one of these cues to release the learned "motive force" that is stored in his memory and the behaviors that result. The child's behaviors that result are an expression of his emotional responses to these environmental cues.

If we go back to our previous example concerning homework instruction — "all I did was ask him if his homework was done and he began to scream, yell, and break things" — we can now understand the child's reaction from the perspective of the learning model. The words of the parent did not cause the explosion.

What happened instead was that the parent's words triggered an emotionally laden learning history. The child's explosion was an emotional reaction that he has learned from previous negative experiences with parents and homework, i.e., his learning history.

The Learning Model vs. the Educational Model

The learning model is often confused with the educational model. The educational model is a constricted subset of the learning model, and thereby its application often leads to very different outcomes. Since it is important not to get the two confused, we need to compare and contrast the two.

The underlying assumption of the educational model is based on skills and is what I call disability by deficit — meaning, if there is problem with a child, then there must be some skills deficit.

Implicit in this notion is that I am a reasonable person and we live in a reasonable world. Therefore, the demands the world and I make on the child are reasonable. So if he does not behave the way I want, then there is something wrong with him. He must have a deficit, as in Attention DEFICIT Disorder.

Since educators are in the business of teaching skills, they logically conclude the deficit must be in skills. Teaching skills is something educators know how to do. Skills, such as making choices, listening, learning to relax, are added to teaching math, reading and social studies skills.

The educational model overlooks the fact that defects can be the result of motivational issues and responses that have been learned too well. If we view these as primal causes of the problem in the first place, our goal is no longer to pile on more layers, or skills, which the educational model does.

Rather, treatment is based on peeling off the motivational layers, as prescribed by the learning model.

The learning model takes into account all that social scientists have discovered about how we learn, which is volumes more that I can touch on here. For our purposes, some of the essential learning issues are motivation, inhibition, emotion, social exchanges, attention, over-learning, and reinforcement schedules.

According to the learning model, problems are understood as learned responses to contingencies, rather than disorganized malfunctions or skills deficits. ADHD is a learned skill in excess.

The Misapplication of Learning and Mechanical Models

If we observe the way parents yell at their children, we can see another example of the misapplication of the mechanical model versus the learning model.

Some parents seem to regard yelling as an efficient method of producing action in their child because initially children do go into action when the parent yells. That's because the child associates more volume with an impending consequence.

The parent, however, believes in the mechanical model and attributes the child's response to the power of their yelling. This may sound silly, but I have had many a mother explain to me that her children mind her husband better because he has a deeper and louder voice when he yells.

This misperception soon breaks down. If a consequence is not forthcoming, the child quickly learns that yelling is "the sound of fury signifying nothing." So, he stops responding to it.

The parent, implicitly believing in the mechanical model, yells louder in the belief that the energy in the yell will be transferred to the child so that action will begin. The response of the child again increases.   Over time, his response will again wane to non-responsiveness. The cycle is repeated, usually over and over, until the yelling in the household is overwhelming and the child's responsiveness is underwhelming.

The child's learning history continues to power his offending behavior.   And the power of the parent's voice ends up powering nothing at all.

The real reason most children respond better to their fathers is that fathers are quicker to back their words with consequences. When mothers learn to do likewise, they also earn responsiveness from their children.

Parents who believe in the mechanical model also talk about their children not hearing them, even though they obviously hear their friends, the teacher, and the call to dinner.   Sometimes the parents will even resort to a medical examination of the child's hearing.

Unlike the mechanical model, the learning model probably has no domain-specific roots built into the structure of our brains.   Therefore, it is not as intuitive. The learning model is the result of slow and detailed study, mostly by psychologists, of animal and human experiments. We have to work to use the learning model, whereas the mechanical model feels natural and easy.   The tendency is to slip back into the mechanical model, even when we know, at a rational level, it is not applicable.

In a demanding and scratchy voice, Scott's mother said, "Scott, you know you have homework. Do you have it done yet? You know how bad you are doing in school. You know if you would just work a little harder you could get good grades." She continued like this until Scott exploded, because, only after he exploded, was she sure Scott had heard her words.

This ritual happened every night, but the time it took Scott to explode got less and less each night.   That's because Scott's mother was training him to anticipate her diatribe.   As he would listen to her speak, his mental cassette tape of what she was going to say sped through his head at lightning fast speed. The faster he learned to do this, the sooner he exploded and the sooner she stopped her lecture.

The explosion was therefore negatively reinforced because it ended her tirade. When I explained the effect of this sequence to Scott's mother, she argued, from the mechanical model, that "He needs to know what is wrong and what to do. If I don't get on him, he won't do anything."

Clearly, she thought of her son as not understanding the problem and not having the energy to resolve it. Her plan was to be that previously mentioned cue ball that would bump him hard enough and in the right direction.

No matter what I suggested, she retorted, "I have tried that and it doesn't work." In a simplistic sense, based on the mechanical model, it did not work.

She would try a new strategy a time or two, and if it did not get automatic results, she would abandon it. She was only able to see Scott's responses in relation to the immediate forces — her acting on him.

In the context of his learning history, there was no way she was going to get the result she wanted.

Though I was eventually able to logically persuade her of the merits of a program shaping a new behavior in her son, until I was able to extinguish her emotional involvement in this pattern, she was unable to follow through with it on daily life.

To make the changes, both of their emotional triggers from their historically destructive sequence had to be eliminated through CAER. Once this was done, it was easy to shape a new learning history.

Chapter 17

The Learning Model and The Behavior Amplifier Effect

Emotional Draw of the Mechanical Model

Obviously, we are often emotionally aroused by ADHD children's antics. In this emotionally aroused state, like the ADHD child, our ability to think of the most effective strategy is limited. We simply are not in a thinking mode, so thinking about what the psychologist told us to do or what we read in a book is far away. Therefore, we act on what is intuitive, the mechanical model, rather than what we have learned is most effective. Later, when we are no longer emotionally aroused, we can see our error.

Even with extensive training in alternate, more accurate reactions, highly educated professionals tend to revert to the mechanical model.

Research in teacher training is a good example of this. Despite training in the developmental concepts of Piaget and Vgyotski and after correctly answering exam questions about them, teachers soon reverted to a simple, domain specific, information-processing model when stressed.

Instead of describing their teaching procedures in terms of the developmental tasks of the children of the age they are working with, they describe packaging the information into bite-size chunks so that children can digest it more easily. This is a domain-specific, intuitive model known as the alimentary model (Hirshfield & Gelman, 1994). The alimentary model, as its name implies, is patterned after our own eating and digestive processes.

Confusion Between Mechanical and Learning Models

The convergence between these models in new situations that have no learning history perpetuates the confusion between them. That's because, at that "new situation" point, no learning has taken place to make behavior any different between the learning and mechanical models.

After time has passed and a learning history has developed, actions based on each of the two models will produce very different results. The hapless and indiscriminate blend of these two models regularly leads to misunderstanding of the ADHD child's antics.

For example, in a new school, many ADHD children behave well for the first few weeks. After they develop a learning history with the teacher and the other students, they once again begin to misbehave.

We must continually remind ourselves that the intuitive appeal of the mechanical model has nothing to do with its effectiveness in dealing with ADHD children. The learning model works much better to explain and change thoughts, feelings, and behavior.

You may not be pushing the button you think you are

Treatment Implications of the Mechanical vs. Learning Model

With the ADHD child, in this mechanical model, the stimulant medications given him help suppress the angry and fearful feelings stored in his mind. But they do not change how he understands his world, i.e. his learning history.

If he did not like math before the medication, he still does not like math after the medication. The stimulant medications just allow him to persevere in spite of the bad feelings triggered by math.

Using the learning model, on the other hand, interventions are designed to change the underlying patterns, which leads to improved functioning for both the child and the environment around him. The actual learned patterns in the child's mind are modified to work better. The essence of the pattern is changed not just its expression.

The biggest difficulty in applying the learning model is that, most of it is invisible. One has to decode the child's learning history through special procedures.

This is done by careful observation of the temporal sequences of stimuli and behaviors, i.e. behavioral analysis. The learning model emphasizes these temporal relationships between events.

By being alert to the timing of events, one can begin to decode the learned relationships between stimuli and responses. Learning history and the resultant behaviors of the ADHD child play out before you. You observe what stimuli the child has learned to respond to, with what behaviors, for what consequences (punishment or rewards).

These behaviors can be words, feelings, thoughts, physiological changes or bodily actions. While these sequences unfold, you can also ask questions about the child's internal experiences, feelings, and thoughts.

Without question, you will find that feelings serve as an intervening variable, that is, outside stimuli encroaching on the child cause him to experience internal feelings. The child then responds behaviorally or mentally to resolve that feeling.

For example, the ADHD child may feel anxious when he sees the week's spelling list. The anxious feeling is resolved by shifting his attention to something else more pleasant like fantasy or play. Being mentally checked out from the classroom, he may get up and wander around or poke someone.

The Behavior Amplifier: The Mechanical Model Obscures the Learning

Once the child starts emitting "inappropriate" behaviors, feedback loops develop between the adult and the child. These loops serve as amplifiers of each other's negative behaviors toward the other, i.e. behavioral amplifiers.

Though both the adult and child are trying to break out of this destructive loop (by changing the other person), their very efforts only fuel the behaviors they are wanting to stop.

Typically, the ADHD child will try to reduce his emotional pain through attentional avoidance, acting out or physical escape. And the teacher or parent, trying to immediately change the child's behavior, will become more demonstrative. The teacher might say, "Sit down and do your work," in a stern and demanding voice.

These efforts by the teacher, though well intended, are usually seen by the child as punishment, and they thereby provide more motivation to further attentionally escape (Danforth, et. al. 1991).

The Solution Becomes the Problem

These emotional feedback loops are unpleasant for both adult and child. Each party intensifies their behavior in an effort to end their own negative emotional experience.

Because of this high level of emotional arousal involved, neither party can think clearly about what will work with the other person. Because of this high emotional arousal, these strategies are based on the intuitive mechanical model rather than the learning model. Thus, they are misdirected and tend to backfire.

Each tries to assert more emotional force on the other through anger, avoidance, crying, yelling, or pouting. Consequently, the very effort each makes to stop the unpleasant exchange is exactly what triggers further escalation of the other's behavior. And the solution becomes the problem.

As described by the Conditioned Attentional Avoidance Loop Model, the child's performance is further reduced, which garners more negative feedback, and so on. A destructive, vicious cycle develops between the adult and child. That's because the true, interactive nature of learning is obscured by the high emotions of the situation.

The problem is that action is applied to the current and visible variables (mechanical model), but the provocative response is grounded in the invisible learning history (learning model) of the other party. This misconception makes the inhibition of provocative behavior difficult for all concerned. As a result, a destructive behavior amplifier has been constructed. And, at the behavioral level, this quickly increases the original, minor deviant behavior into something diagnosable.

How Adults are Seduced into The Conditioned Attentional Avoidance Loop

Clearly adults are an integral part of the Conditioned Attentional Avoidance Loop surrounding the child, but less clear is why adults continue to "choose" to participate in this destructive exchange.

Of course, they do not "choose" any more than the child does. The dynamics we have discussed in the child's case work just as well for the adults. In the same sense, it works for adults in two ways.

First, when pressed by adults, children will satisfy adults need to know the "why" behind the child's behavior.

They generate post hoc answers tailored to satisfy the immediate adult demand.

Secondly, adult pressure on the child often serves to suppress his immediate acting out, which reduces his current aversiveness to the adult.

Authority figures in the child's environment are seduced into continuing their strategies, for three reasons.

First, "a talking to" to the child will often elicit the positive, promise-to-be-compliant words the adult is looking for. We are all inclined to respond to the words that we want to hear as if they are the reality they represent.

Second, punishment often succeeds in providing the adult with immediate control of the child's behavior, that is, cessation of the child's annoying behavior, which negatively reinforces the authority figure's punishing behavior.

Increased punishment of undesirable behavior temporarily motivates the child to meet the demand and apply willful controls to his attention. The effect is temporary because eventually the child learns to blot out negative stimuli at a higher level through attentional avoidance at a higher level.

Third, teachers know and are given few other tools to deal with what amounts to an impossible situation.

Sean, a 14-Year-Old ADHD Adolescent

Irate parents will often bring their children to me after he has made the "final transgression." Sean, a 14-year-old, was dragged into my office after he had been expelled from school for taking a marijuana pipe to class.

His mother had asked him, "Are you smoking pot? Why did you take that thing to school? What am I going to do with you?"

Sean's initial answer was to all her questions was, "I dunno."

Since that did not satisfy his mother, she kept grilling him. He finally came up with a story that stopped the questioning. He told her he was "keeping it for a friend so that he wouldn't get in trouble." Sean's mother didn't really buy the story, but at least she had an answer. So she stopped interrogating her son.

Sean told me what really happened. He said that for a few months he and a friend had gotten into the habit of walking a back way to school and smoking pot along the way. The grass helped him "get through Mr. Garvin's social studies class, and nobody was hurt."

He had also gotten in the habit of tossing the pipe in the bottom of his book bag. One day, after he had pretty much forgotten about the pipe, he began looking through his book bag for his math homework. And the pipe flipped out of the bag.

The real problem was not the pot or the pipe. The real problem was that Sean and his friend found their classes so aversive that they had to find some way to get through them more comfortably.

Their parents might have chosen Ritalin for them. Sean and his friend chose marijuana because it was what was available.

The solution was to use no drugs at all. Eliminating Sean's negative emotional responses to school and school work through family therapy and setting up a positive reward system for good school behavior and grades made drugs of any sort, irrelevant.

Chapter 18

The Effects of the Broader Cultural Context

The behavior problems of the ADHD child do not happen just because of the interpersonal reactions that come their way from their immediate environment. Psychological and cultural forces effect behavior in profound ways. We will look at the function, mechanisms, intensity and quality of the socialization process and its affect on the ADHD problem.

Emotional Contagion: a Mechanism for Socialization

I remember my first observation of emotional contagion. It was in 8th grade. A high jump pit was built on the playground. A handful of the athletic boys would take turns jumping over it, one after the other. The rest of us nerds would stand around in a group and watch intently.

One day I noticed that almost all of the spectators would synchronously raise one leg a few inches above the ground as each jumper leaped over the bar. I also noticed how hard it was not to raise my leg in time with each jumper.

If I did not consciously and specifically inhibit the response, if I let my mind wander, my leg automatically went up — just the way it did with 30 other boys. In fact, it was a rather funny sight, watching 30 kids standing around in a group simultaneously, repeatedly raising one leg every few minutes.

Contrary to current rhetoric, the causes of our feelings are broader than just our own responsibility. Many of our feelings arise from our interactions with those around us. We are as much a reflection of our group and culture as we are of our own self-determination (Mischel, 1968). Emotional contagion is one of our most basic social processes and is at the root of much of our feelings and behavior. We can see this from our earliest social engagements.

> *From a few months after birth through the first year of life, studies have shown, infants react to the pain of others as though it were happening to themselves. Seeing another child hurt and start crying, they themselves begin to cry, especially if the other child cries for more than a minute or two. (Goleman, 1989, p. B1)*

Around one year of age, infants begin to realize that the distress is being felt by someone else.

> *They recognize it's the other kid's problem, but they are often confused over what to do about it... (Goleman, 1989, p. B1)*

During this phase, toddlers often imitate the distress of someone else — apparently, researchers say, in an effort to understand better what the other person is feeling.

> *"From around 14 months to 2 or 2 1/2 years, you see children feel their own fingers to see if they hurt when someone else hurts their fingers," says Miron Radk-Yarrow, chief of the Laboratory of Developmental Psychology at the National Institute of Mental Health. "By 2 1/2, though, toddlers clearly realize that someone else's pain is different from their own, and know how to comfort them appropriately."* (Goleman, 1989, p. B1)

The Contagion Effect of Depression

Parents have an equally strong emotional effect on their children. "When a mother is distressed, if her body stiffens, the infant in her stiffened arms will also experience distress." (Fisher & Fisher, 1994, p 84)

Infants and toddlers of depressed mothers are at risk of depression themselves because of the depressed affect communicated to them (Downey & Coyne, 1990). In the same vein, children who view adults expressing extreme anger become more aggressive toward their peers (Cummings, 1987). Clearly young children respond to the depression and anger expressed by their parents.

These same effects have also been well-documented in interactions between adults. Talking to or living with a depressed person can make one more depressed.

In one such experiment, college men were asked to call and talk to a specific woman for 20 minutes. Unbeknownst to them, they were assigned to call either a depressed woman or a non- depressed woman.

This interaction had a clear impact on the men. After the conversation, men who talked to the depressed woman felt more depressed, anxious, and hostile than they had prior to their conversation, especially when compared to the men who talked to a non-depressed woman. (Hatfield, et. al., 1992)

In another, rather disturbing experiment, college students were assigned either a mildly depressed or non-depressed roommate. Those who lived with the depressed roommate became progressively more depressed over time (Coyne, 1976).

Crowd Contagion

Crowd behavior and mass hysteria are another powerful variation of the emotional contagion phenomenon. Throughout the world we see examples of this. Sometimes this contagious emotion is laughing and crying as has been observed in East African tribesmen (Ebrahim 1968).

In the New Guinea Highlanders, researchers have documented group acts of sexual acting out, giddiness, and anger (Reay, 1960). Physical symptoms such as seizures, trance states, screaming, crying, sweating, flailing of arms and legs, dizziness, numbness, and faintness spread among factory workers in Singapore in 1973 (Chew, Phoon, & Mae-Lim, 1976).

Emotional contagion is a very primitive and powerful form of interpersonal communication.

Hatfield describes "emotional contagion [as] that which is relatively automatic, unintentional, uncontrollable, and largely inaccessible to conversant awareness (1994, p.5)." "[It is] the tendency to automatically mimic and synchronize facial expressions, vocalizations, postures, and movements with those of another person and, consequently, to converge [with them] emotionally." (Hatfield, et. al., 1992, p 153-154)

How Emotional Contagion Works

Emotional contagion is accounted for by two mechanisms:

1) *"People do tend automatically to mimic or synchronize with the facial expressions, vocal expressions, postures, and movements of those around them...."*

2) And, *"People tend to experience emotions consistent with the facial, vocal and postural expressions they adopt."* *"Evidence from a variety of disciplines, including animal research, developmental psychology, clinical psychology and social psychology [indicates] that such emotional contagion is pervasive."* *(Hatfield, et. al, 1994, p. 6)*

These responses are not under conscious control or awareness but are a function of basal brain structures (Davis, 1985). If this is the case, then emotions are not just an individual's responsibility or a choice. We must address a wider array of causes that are responsible for our emotions.

Emotional contagion is clearly evident in our daily language. When we hear someone's sad story we say, "I feel for you," meaning I can empathetically feel some of your distress. When parents spank their children, they often say, "This hurts me more than it does you," which translates as my cognitive knowledge of parenting dictates that I must do this to you, but to do it I must also feel your (the child's) pain.

When someone is physically injured, observers will often say something like, "I could just feel how much that hurt."

All of this sounds very similar to the empathetic discomfort, discussed above, that young children feel towards another child's discomfort.

Which Illusion?

Children no longer live in little self-contained, controlled worlds where perceptions, values, feelings, and thoughts can be systematically distorted for the cultural good.

From their earliest years, they are bombarded with diverse and contradictory sets of values, emotions, religions, worldviews, and behaviors. These make it much more difficult for them to feret out a workable, culturally acceptable illusory system.

That's because these conflicting inputs, images, and messages draw children, and adults for that matter, in a multitude of opposing directions. Without a few organizing principles to sort the meaningful from the empty, the useful from the wasteful, children chart a very jagged course.

This shows up in the incongruent behavior we see in children, particularly those labeled ADHD. One minute they will be having a rational, adult conversation with you, the next they are fighting and yelling. From their culturally socialized experience of continual incongruence, there is nothing of concern in this disjointed stream of behaviors.

Parents are Slacking Off

Parents often provide little guidance in developing these central-organizing principles. According to A.C. Nielson Co., "The average American parent spends 3.5 minutes per week engaged in meaningful conversation with his children. The average child, however, spends 1,680 minutes per week watching television." (Spokesman-Review, 4/29/96, Page B5)

It is easy to see why, from the child's perspective, input from television comes with as much or more validity and authority than a parent's admonitions. If parents only spend 3.5 minutes per week in meaningful conversation with their children, we are wasting our time addressing child behavior problems by trying to change cultural parenting practices. It would seem that the only way to change the child's values is to change television.

Of course, for the individual troubled child brought to therapy by concerned parents, I am making an exaggeration. But for the population at large, it is no exaggeration at all.

In general, parents are not performing their parental roles. The family television and the program producers and advertisers behind television are raising our children, i.e. a child's behavior is often patterned after what the television models for him.

The Cultural Context of the Socialization Process

Our thoughts, feelings, and behaviors are directed as much by our images as the realities they represent. Some of these images are carefully cultured illusions.

> *One of the most basic aspects of socialization, namely, the transmission of values, requires an elaborate and skilled exercise of make-believe on the part of children, who are the targets of the whole process. They must adapt to the illusion that the culture knows what is correct and right. (Fisher & Fisher, 1993, p. 95)*

> *Children probably cannot enter their culture unless they master the intricacies of the rules defining its pattern of unrealities. It would*

appear, too, that the rigid impulse controls demanded by cultures require a cognitive "compartment," where illusory images can be generated. (Fisher & Fisher 1993, p. 98)

One of those compartments is the hard plastic case of the television set. To interact with this compartment, little energy has to be expended. Nothing has to be generated. Only passive absorption is required. Nothing could be easier and more seductive. Given the conflicting values in his environment, what images of correct behavior should the child generate? The choice of what to pretend and what to do is diverse and inconsistent.

Does one identify with the illusion one sees on TV, what parents say, what parents do, what teachers say, what teachers do, what peers think...? Illusion is a useful mechanism if there is a culturally tested and prescriptive formula for what to pretend. Otherwise it is just another mechanism to pull the child in many contradictory directions.

Nevertheless, the ability to pretend is such an important activity for children that as a culture we should not abandon harnessing it as a powerful adaptive mechanism.

There are multiple research reports indicating that the ability to pretend and imagine is associated with the ability to be reflective rather than impulsive, to exercise self-control rather than seek immediate gratification. The capacity to create pretend fantasies apparently provides a buffer against immediate motoric expression of feelings and impulses. It has been observed that the more children can and do engage in pretend play, the more controlled [and] "law abiding" is their overt behavior (Fisher & Fisher, 1993, p. 96).

However, this is not a simple linear relationship. The effectiveness of pretend-based control of impulsive behavior has its limits. Beyond a certain point, illusion becomes dissociation. Nothing is controlled because that which should be controlled is dissociated out of consciousness.

Once the impulse has moved beyond being directed into fantasy and on to separation from conscious, there is little to contain it. Like many mechanisms there is an optimum mid-range value. High or low extreme values are dysfunctional.

In addition:

> *Pretense provides an unusual opportunity for children to control their own emotional arousal and to maintain a level that is both comfortable and stimulating. The intrinsic motivation of pretense resides in its ability to convert external sources of motivation. (Fein, 1981, p. 301)*

One aspect of ADHD happens when this ability to pretend is taken to such an extreme that it begins to backfire.

The attentional avoidance ("pretense," in Fein's terms) initially helps children keep their emotional experience of the cultural demands in the classroom "at a level that is both comfortable and stimulating." But a problem arises when this strategy interacts with the structured performance demands of the classroom. When the two meet, conflict, obviously, is created. This conflict eventually evolves into the detrimental Conditioned Attentional Avoidance Loop. ADHD is a child's extreme extension of their natural use of pretense to help them adapt to cultural demands.

The TV has ADHD Too!

Television, cartoons, movies, and comic books clearly and repeatedly enact all of the behaviors that we associate with ADHD — sudden, self-expressive movements; impulsive speaking out; angry affect; quick and aggressive movements; aggressively standing up for one's rights, not simply assertively; and rebellion toward authority.

Strip ADHD of its medical-sounding language and these are apt descriptors for ADHD. The child does not have to invent antisocial behaviors. The media provides everything he needs to know about becoming ADHD, and the child has only to model what he sees. It is not just the child who has ADHD, the media does too.

Clearly, the effect of emotional contagion can be seen if we consider television programs. The child is only modeling what he sees beautiful, powerful, high social status, rich people doing. Isn't that what most of us do?

Research proves that children exposed to these models are likely to adopt the characters' antisocial ways of thinking and behavior as their own (Higgins, 1989). When one considers this, it is not surprising how many children act out in school — they are only continuing what they have seen in the media and at home. If their parents or the cartoon characters hit each other, interrupt in conversations, or yell, why shouldn't they do likewise?

Teachers in an Impossible Emotional Bind

These cultural problems also have had a negative influence on our schools. As the family has degenerated, schools, media, peers, the legal system and government have taken over parental roles. And, specifically, criticizing the educational system — teachers, curriculum, funding, etc. — has been a current national pastime.

The monster we criticize, though, was created by the surreal and incompatible demands we place on schools. As the culture has progressively redefined the task of schools, it has increasingly become their responsibility not just to teach the 3R's but to direct this socialization process.

It is the difficulty in shouldering this socialization task, not teaching the 3R's, that has led to our current predicament with public education. One of the problems with this migration of responsibilities is that we have not equipped schools to handle it. We require the schools to be parents without authorizing schools to use the same range of contingencies that parents have traditionally employed.

Loss of Core Self Inhibitory Skills

What relevance does this have to ADHD?

In the critical early years of development, children are not learning appropriate self-inhibitory skills. Core personality development necessary for effective functioning in this culture is not being developed. For example, today's children have little reflexive respect for authority. A frown by an adult does not elicit the response it did forty years ago.

My mother-in-law tells the story of weekly visits to her grandparents where she and her two sisters were required to sit on the couch in silence for two or three hours while the adults conversed. One cannot imagine such an event occurring in the 1990s. What makes it worse is that today's child, because of exposure to the media, continues to absorb antisocial impulses to the exclusion of those internally developed inhibitions required by the school setting.

Unlike past eras, the culturally grounded, self-inhibition patterns are not instilled in the child, so the teacher cannot use them to control behavior and motivate performance. In effect, the teachers do not have the building blocks the child needs to assemble appropriate classroom behavior. Rather, the teacher's standards run into conflict with the counter productive emotional training many of these ADHD children bring to school.

As well, the 6-year-old is confronted with the limitations of one adult teaching 20 or 30 children at a time. And the school staff is saddled with the responsibility of controlling this rowdy mess of emotionally provocative children, but they are not allowed the tools that have been available to parents for thousands of years.

By some form of magic, teachers are supposed to do what the parents have left undone and the media has further provoked.

Teachers Have Narrow Options to Control Disruptive Behavior

When dealing with inattentive or disruptive kids, the options teachers have to punish or reinforce are narrow. About all they can do is constantly tell the child to do his work and sit in his desk. If things really get out of hand, they can send the child to the counselor or principal to "have a talking to."

This consistent, low-level nagging by teachers is one of the engines driving the development of ADHD. That's because the ADHD child can easily tune out nagging.

To be truly effective, the teacher must either get the child's attention or stop annoying him. The way to get his attention is through sufficiently strong punishment. Otherwise, his avoidance skills are just enhanced.

In fact, inducing occasional, well-timed unhappiness in their offspring is what good parents have been doing for millenia. And they know that can be a very effective parenting strategy.

But when the teacher has neither adequate contingencies at her disposal nor is able to tap into the child's prior emotional conditioning, the result is ugly.

The child may simply drop out or be expelled from school if he is unable to inhibit the expression of antisocial values. If he can muster enough inhibition to remain in the school setting, then he may develop ADHD, Learning Disabilities or Behavior Disabilities.

Inspiration in the Classroom: Teachers in an Impassible Bind

There can also be a positive side to emotional contagion. We call it charisma and inspiration. Think about the teachers who inspired and motivated you. For me, they were the ones who expressed their own personal enthusiasm for the subject. Not only did they teach, they shared their excitement. And, through emotional contagion, we experienced their excitement.

Today, we want teachers to offer the same inspiring and dynamic experience for our students' academic and emotional development. But, because of the generalized inhibition required in schools, we put the teacher and the student in an impossible double bind.

We require them to inhibit their emotional responsiveness, which forces them into being professional robots. They are forced into the contradiction of being emotionally inspiring machines.

Generalized Inhibition in the Classroom

Inhibition is not selective enough to permit emotionally dynamic and inspiring teaching while, at the same time, forcing teachers to restrain their negative emotional responses that ADHD students chronically provoke. In a classroom of diverse children, the emotional responsiveness necessary to inspire some, at the same time, will trigger in others the behavior amplifier that was discussed earlier.

Therefore, while inspiring higher performing children, the teachers are likely to be stimulating feelings of failure in those who cannot perform at that level.

Conversely, if the teacher is trying to inhibit the ADHD child, it will be very difficult to inspire the more productive child.

Besides trying to respond to children's needs in this emotionally jumbled collage, teachers have to be constantly, consciously, self-monitoring to make sure that they do not violate one of the school's rules of "liability reduction" — don't yell, don't touch, don't get angry, don't work them too hard, don't give too much homework, don't be affectionate, don't hug, don't be too stern, don't make any parent angry.

Teachers always have to be their own observer. To do this, they must remain a little dissociated from the situation. This dissociation further emotionally distances them from genuine emotional communications with their students.

After teachers are emotionally sanitized, they are given no significant reinforcers or punishers. Yet, through some sort of voodoo, they are supposed to keep 30 children happy, learning, and in their seats. Some of these 30 children need tender loving care and support, others need intellectual inspiration, and others need firm discipline.

These children require and stimulate a wide range of emotional responses from the teacher. It is an impossible demand to ask the teachers at one moment to be attentive, caring, and tender to one child and the next minute to be sternly disciplining to another child.

Being an instantly changing emotional chameleon does not work for the teacher or the child. The teacher has to dampen his emotional responding at both ends of the spectrum. The child receives washed out, flattened, overly modulated responses from the teacher. This shadow of a response carries little emotional contagion with it and, therefore, has little impact, good or bad, on the child. We are asking things from our teachers that are far too difficult, and because of this, we set them up to fail.

This emotional flatness often overflows into the teacher's personal life. Some teachers become what

Joseph Campbell called "fillet fish". They cognitively edit everything they say for non-offensiveness and political correctness. They end up being pleasant, but vanilla, passionless people who neither please nor offend. Their spouses sometimes grow bored with this and leave.

Dynamic, inspiring teaching is incompatible with the situational demand for self-inhibition. But, in fact, we do demand both from our teachers. This is grist for the mills of those preoccupied with our national pastime of criticizing the schools. We have engineered an educational catch-22 situation, which then becomes a basis for criticizing the schools for not taking a more aggressive posture on both sides of the double-bind conflict.

We ask, "Why aren't our kids learning more?" and "Why do they let kids get away with that?" Teaching, as we culturally expect it, may be an impossible task.

Generalized Inhibition Harms Children Too

This inhibition of emotional expression, particularly anger, that we require of teachers and children, is costly. Inhibitory responses are non-specific (Logan & Cowan, 1984) and, therefore concurrently, affect everything from heart rate (Jennings et. al. 1992) to arithmetic memory (Zbrodoff & Logan, 1986).

Inhibition affects thoughts, feelings, pulse, gastric motility, fingertip sweating, muscle tension, etc. This means that it is difficult to inhibit the expression of any emotion without also inhibiting a variety of other emotional and physiological responses.

Math, reading, and spelling, which require sequencing and unbroken attention, are very common hurdles for ADHD children because they are more vulnerable to generalized inhibition than are art or music.

Also, the more acquired or learned a skill, the more vulnerable it is to generalized inhibition. This further explains why many children have more difficulty with math, reading, and spelling, which are more learning dependent, than with subjects such as art and music, which are grounded in more expressive and inherent (domain-specific) abilities.

Because it is global in nature, self-inhibition can also affect children motivationally. We want them to be motivated by their schoolwork, while at the same time we want them to inhibit the forces of hyper-agitation endemic to our culture. We can either have motivation (emotional responsiveness), or we can have behavior control (emotional inhibition). We cannot have both in the same situation from the same child.

This situation would seem to call for an innovative strategy. There are severe constraints here too. One has to be innovative without making anyone unhappy. This is both impossible and undesirable. Real innovation invariably makes someone unhappy somewhere. Disgruntled parents and/or their lawyers often challenge the occasional innovative strategy, which is demoralizing for the innovator.

The alternative for the teacher is to suppress, inhibit, and not make waves. The most effective way to do this is just to do nothing, to be as vanilla as possible. If one looks at our educational system, it is obvious that these contingencies have created the vanilla, politically correct tenor of our schools.

Chapter 19

The Evolution of the ADHD Child

ADHD evolves in two different stages. First, the ADHD itself is created. Then it is spread from one situation and person to another.

Creating ADHD

ADHD behavior does not manifest initially in the form we finally recognize and diagnose.

Parents can typically trace ADHD back to early, rudimentary components of the child's behavior. These behaviors grow over time until they reach the threshold for being identified and labeled. In fact, when these behaviors first emerge, they are lower in intensity and have less of an angry, impulsive quality. At this point, most of these behaviors are considered normal. They only become a problem after they increase in intensity and are considered obnoxious to adults, which can happen for a variety of reasons.

Therefore, at the surface, we would point to increased frequency and intensity of the child's behaviors as the driving factor. But in reality, it is the parent's (or teacher's) response to these behaviors that triggers the next stage in this seeming battle of wills between adult and child.

"I have trained this psychologist to give me an M&M every time I press this bar."

The first grader, for example, might start out being out of his seat as often as his peers. Then something happens so that his behavior becomes an issue for the teacher. This might happen because of a random convergence of events in the classroom, a change in teacher sensitivity or escalation in the child's activity.

Whatever the reason, the teacher begins to respond negatively to the child's behavior. That response may speed the growth of ADHD. What started out as an average time out of one's seat is quickly multiplied by a reinforcing positive feedback loop between teacher and child. And for the teacher and child, this becomes a problem when the loop predominates their interaction.

Let's examine some of the more common issues that bring children's behaviors into a negative focus. These include family stress, parental emotional distress, personality conflict between adult and child, random variation in the child's behavior and environmental sensitivity, and conflicting cultural values.

The Personality Conflict Trigger

At times there are quite specific personality conflicts between a child and his caretaker. In such situations, each is treading on the sensitivities of the other. Rather than being the products of the situation, these sensitivities are usually part of the learning history brought to the situation by each individual. An example might be a child from an emotional, outspoken, verbal, action-oriented family who is taught by a constrained, proper, quiet, emotionally unexpressive teacher.

The teacher is very likely to find the child's behavior, which is considered normal and functional at home, abrasive, rude, and uncontrolled. Although the teacher may try to mask his feelings about the child's behavior, the child is probably aware of the teacher's feelings toward him — via emotional contagion (Hatfield, Cacioppo & Rapson, 1994). The child is then mobilized by the teacher's aversion to him and the Conditioned Attentional Avoidance Loop begins.

These types of personality conflicts are not strictly individual variations. In a culture as increasingly diverse as ours, where the educator and the student are often of different subcultures, such personality conflicts may be cultural conflicts. They then represent a difference in the values and behaviors of a subculture. This may be why there is a higher representation of ADHD among the poor and some subculture families.

Karl, an ADHD Boy

Though the chain of events leading to Karl's ADHD could have been interrupted, no one is to blame for the fact that Karl developed ADHD.

First grade went well for him. But in second grade, he and his family moved, and Karl had to enter a new school where he had no friends.

The move was particularly disruptive because it happened about a month into second grade and caused him to miss almost two weeks of class. This left him distracted and a little behind. That, in combination with a teacher who had a slightly harsher style than Karl was used to, started the feedback loop and his downward spiral.

Karl didn't get his work done in class, so his teacher kept him in at recess to finish. Karl was daydreaming a bit about his former home and school. He sometimes did this in class and during his recess catch-up sessions.

Two things happened at that point. He discovered that it was more pleasant to fantasize about his old home, friends and school than it was to deal with his new schoolwork. This negatively reinforced his fantasizing strategy. And, since he was fantasizing, he was not efficient at work, so Karl spent more and more recesses trying to catch up.

After many months of falling behind in schoolwork and spending his recesses making up class work, he began to dislike his teacher and school. He was constantly under pressure and did not have any fun. As well, a mutual antagonism developed between Karl and his teacher. There were subtle non-verbal looks and gestures between them that transmitted their discomfort with each other.

The teacher sometimes impatiently interrupted Karl when he asked a question. Sometimes Karl glowered at her. Not only was he spending many recesses doing work, but he began to dislike the math that most often filled his recess time. And, he began to dislike anything that reminded him of math.

In fact, during math, Karl always had a tense feeling in his stomach. At first, his mind was busy with phrases like, "Math sucks," "I am really dumb," "Other kids know how dumb I am," and "I hate Mr. Feldon." These statements made Karl feel even worse.

Over time, the statements and images that made him feel bad were replaced with far away thoughts that made him feel better — again his old home, his old school, his dog, building a model plane, playing a computer game. Since these thoughts made Karl feel better, they became stronger, more frequent, and more automatic. Pretty soon math was not nearly so bad because it was not nearly there.

This frustrated Mr. Feldon. He really wanted to help Karl turn around his declining academic performance. He worked harder to remind Karl to get back to work when he was inattentive or not accomplishing much. He instructed his aid to do likewise. But to Karl, it seemed like they were "always on me." It broke his pleasant fantasies and put him back in contact with the annoying schoolwork.

Since Mr. Feldon and his aid were instrumental in making Karl feel bad, he began to dislike them even more, which motivated him to fantasize more. Soon Karl was spending a few hours a week outside the classroom with a special education teacher. At first, Karl liked the special education teacher, but soon she began to irritate him just as much as Mr. Feldon did.

As Karl's academic problems worsened, he began acting out his frustration and resentment on his peers and occasionally in the classroom.

A conference was scheduled with his parents. They reported that he had also been disruptive at home, fighting with his siblings and mouthing off to his parents. The school counselor suggested that Karl might be ADHD. His parents were referred to a pediatrician for an evaluation. After interviewing Karl and his family and administering a behavior checklist to the parents, the pediatrician diagnosed Karl as ADHD. He recommended Ritalin.

The parents were not willing to put their son on drugs, so they asked about other treatments. This resulted in Karl's referral to my office for CAER treatment. CAER was effective for Karl and his family. Until CAER treatment, the harder everyone tried to help Karl, the more his problem was aggravated. A "personality clash" instigated the Conditioned Attentional Avoidance Loop, then it escalated and spread through most contexts in Karl's life. No one was to blame, but everyone contributed to his problem.

Family Stress

Family stress includes events such as a new baby, illness, financial changes, substance abuse, marital conflict, and other problems that tax the family's emotional and behavioral resources. Families subject to these stressing events have less tolerance for discordant behavior, and the family functions the way individuals function — how does your personal tolerance for irritating or frustrating events change when you are tired or stressed out?

Most people are much less tolerant and forgiving when they are exhausted. This can be seen in a tired mother, just home from work, who finds her child's room dirty. Normally this would elicit a minor reprimand. But in her exhausted state her tolerance is reduced, so she yells and grounds him for a month.

Any stress added to the system can elicit a response far out of proportion. This added sensory load may be a child out of his seat at school, a game played too loudly at home, or sibling battles.

The impact of the adult's exhaustion, frustration, anger and overreaction is every bit as powerful in shaping the child's behavior as more appropriate emotional responses. To the child, only the parent's response is important, whether intended or not. Thus, the adults' emotional displays shape the development of ADHD. Saying "I'm sorry" or "I didn't mean it" offers little help.

Learned Hypersensitivity to Subtle Cues

I was always careful to listen to my father's steps as he walked through the house. If the floor creaked more and his steps were faster, I knew there was little chance I could go through the main part of the house without getting yelled at for something. To avoid being yelled at, I would use the outside door to my bedroom and escape his wrath.

I also learned that if he sat a little more hunched he was soon going to get mad at me for something. Sometimes the silent tension in anticipation of the yelling was so strong that tears would just start streaming down my cheeks. At this point, my mother would intervene in the unspoken drama and allow me to go to my room.

At the time, it would have been difficult for me to articulate what the cues were that I was responding to. I just knew that at certain times I felt terrible. It was only at about 17-years-old, when I was about to leave home, did I begin to figure out more specifically what triggered these bad feelings.

Teachers Cannot Help Being Part of the Behavior Amplifier

The mutually learned sensitivities between child and adult increase over time. The interpersonal cues can be subtle and brief. A look, a gesture, or a voice tone may be enough to trigger an emotional and/or attentional response.

In general, "It doesn't take much of people's expressions, voices, or actions for others to pick up on what they are feeling." (Hatfield, Cacioppo, Rapson, 1994, p. 129)

The same is clearly true in the classroom. Ambadly and Rosenthal (1992), in their research, demonstrated that children can accurately assess their teachers' feelings toward them with minimal cues. This hypersensitivity to subtle cues has similarly been demonstrated in children observing their mothers and in jurors observing trial lawyers and judges.

We have all experienced this hypersensitivity to cues from people close to us. We can all remember how we as children could tell from the slightest cue if our parents were mad. We might have noticed the change in the rhythm of their walk, a look, or a change of voice tone. Later in life, we are likely to have developed the same hypersensitivity to the cues our spouse or our boss sends.

The Behavior Amplifier in Action

The feelings, behaviors, and attention of children, parents, and teachers are driven by very similar subtle social cues. Over time, they all learn to respond quicker to each other's cues. Subtler and subtler cues set off these chain reactions. As the ADHD scene is repeated over and over, with slight variations, it becomes more standard, repetitious, and habitual. The participants begin to get the feeling that they have done this before and before and before. This means that despite the efforts of teachers to be, in their words, "professional," they cannot hide their feelings from their students. They cannot avoid being part of the behavior amplifier.

Chapter 20

The Power of Labels

Labels Create a Self-fulfilling Prophecy

Labels have the power to directly shape the behavior that is assigned to them. Once the word is out that Jason is ADHD, he lives up to his diagnosis — for himself and others. I'll illustrate with a study.

It has long been known that attractive people make more positive first impressions. It turns out that these impressions can have a powerful effect on behavior.

Men were asked to have a 10-minute telephone conversation with a woman whose picture they had been given. The picture, however, was not of the women with whom they talked with. When the men were given a picture of attractive woman rather than homely woman, the conversation was quite different.

In essence, during the short span of a telephone conversation, the women became what men expected. The women who were believed to be attractive became more animated, confident, and adept. By contrast, the women whom the men believed were homely became more withdrawn, lacking in confidence, and awkward (Hatfield & Sprecher, 1986).

These changes in the women's behavior were directly related to how men talked with them.

> *[Men] who thought they were talking to beautiful women were more sociable, sexually warm, interesting, independent, sexually permissive, bold, outgoing, humorous, and socially adept than the men who thought they were talking to homely women. The men assigned to 'attractive' women were also more comfortable, enjoyed themselves more, liked their partners more, took the initiative more often, and used their voices more effectively. In a nutshell, the men who thought they had attractive partners tried harder. Undoubtedly, this behavior caused the women to try harder in return. If the stereotypes held by men became reality within only 10 minutes of telephone conversation, one can imagine what happens over several years. (Hatfield, et. al., 1994, p. 114-115)*

The ADHD Label Shapes Behavior

If we place the teacher in the role of the men in this study, and the ADHD labeled children in place of the homely women, we may have a better understanding of part of the dynamics that shape the ADHD child's behavior. It would then seem likely that the adults framing the child with "homely" ADHD features would be inclined to bring these characteristics out in the child.

Thus, the adult's perceptions, not just the child's behavior, must be changed.

However, the ADHD diagnosis makes Jason's role much simpler for himself and others since that label allows all to know and agree upon the rules and roles. Diagnostic categories serve as a conceptual rallying point to help achieve consensus on action among the people who work with Jason.

Labeling Transfers the Problem to New Situations

The development and use of labels, such as ADHD, provide a mechanism for the efficient transfer of this pattern to other adults and other children. In a sense, others become infected with ADHD. The child and the adult each have their mechanisms that facilitate the epidemic. The adults use their superior verbal skills to communicate to one another the child's ADHD label. The child generalizes his effective adaptation technique to other situations in which he feels uncomfortable.

Transferring the ADHD Label Between Adults

How adults respond to ADHD behaviors is influenced by the way they talk about it. The behaviors implied by ADHD label provide an organization for the teacher's perception of the child and the way he behaves. The teacher then is more likely to respond to the ADHD and thereby amplify it.

For example, one teacher tells another teacher that the child is ADHD. The new teacher is then sensitized to look for ADHD. But before the child's actions were labeled ADHD, his behaviors were less likely to trigger a response and thereby be reinforced.

ADHD kids intuitively sense this problem and that is the reason they often do not want anyone to know they take Ritalin and often object strongly to having to go to the office to take their noontime tablet.

By contrast, a child's ADHD-like behavior that is not noticed, and thereby does not elicit a response from the environment, is less likely to reoccur. The child will only continue to do what, from his perspective, works, at least in the short term.

Drawing attention to the behaviors increases the probability that they will "work" and, therefore, be reinforced. In this limited sense, if you do not see it, (which is different from ignoring it) it is more likely to go away.

That's why, even though the time-released Ritalin spanuals do not work as well, sometimes it is better to use them. Then the child can avoid being labeled defective and can avoid being shamed for having to take medication.

This is not a prescription for ignoring the child. Many times, "ignoring" the child's label does not work because he can easily detect that this is not genuine. And he really is getting the emotional response he wants from the adult. The size of the adult's emotional display is not what is important. Rather, it is the information it conveys about the adult's emotional state. Only a small vignette of the adult's behavior is necessary to convey the internal state.

An old but clever study demonstrates this quite graphically. Before the beginning of the school year, experimenters manipulated teachers' expectancies about how well some students were anticipated to perform the following year. Then they followed the children's performance over the next year.

The children tended to live up to teacher expectations. Compared to a control group, those who were expected to "bloom" intellectually in fact did. This was most apparent with first and second graders, which is when most ADHD children are identified. (Rosenthal, 1968) Not only do reactions to children labeled with ADHD spread to other adults, the child's behavior spreads across situations.

The Child's Generalization of a Strategy that Works

A parallel strategy works for children. Once a child's emotional patterns are established and work in one situation, be it math or spelling, they tend to spread to other situations that stimulate the same uncomfortable feelings. At first, the problem is only manifest in math or Mrs. Smith's class. Later when he feels uncomfortable in social studies, he begins to use his ADHD skills there. No one really notices at first. But as the strategy works, it spreads until adults begin to notice and label the child as ADHD.

In the same manner, adults sensitized to one ADHD child transfer this to other children who provoke similar feelings in them. Thus, other children who elicit the same feelings in them are likely to be subject to the same strategies applied to the first child. Once the behavior is resonating in one feedback loop, the child and the teacher are both likely to generalize their strategies to other situations and persons.

I remember Ellen, a fourth year elementary school teacher who came for therapy because she was so stressed from teaching. She was thinking about quitting at the end of the year. She loved teaching, but there were a few ADHD children who upset her greatly. Ellen felt helpless and incompetent to deal with them.

She had sought help from her principal and other teachers. Though their advice seemed sound and she resolved to try it, when faced with these children's antics, she became so upset and frustrated that she found herself yelling at them. She knew this wasn't appropriate, but they got to her.

While she was in the CAER machine, we traced back in her personal life and teaching life the feelings the ADHD children in her current class provoked in her. Though there were many small repetitions of these feelings, there seemed to be two primary historical roots to her current experience.

In her first year of teaching, she got "the child from hell." He seemed bent on making her life miserable. She worked with school psychologists, special education teachers, and consultants with no success managing this child. After several months, he was removed from her class and put into a behavior disabilities classroom. Though he was gone, she remained phobic of ever having another child like this.

These feelings of helplessness and frustration also dated back to her childhood when her older brother used to tease and taunt her for hours. Once these historical feelings were extinguished with CAER, her job seemed much more manageable. Though ADHD children were still difficult, Ellen no longer felt helpless and incompetent to deal with them. She continues to be a successful elementary school teacher.

Children train adults and adults train children in ADHD patterns. This is part of the energy behind the current epidemic of ADHD.

The Label Obscures Small Improvements so More Effective Behaviors are Not Shaped

The ADHD label traps the child in another way. Because of his ADHD label, the school and family are sensitive to his diagnosis and the behaviors it implies. Conversely, this means that the parents, teachers, and friends often fail to respond to the incremental improvements brought by treatment.

Many times improvement for these children consists of a reduction in negative behavior, such as moving around less and speaking out less. Today Jason stays in his seat for 10 minutes instead of his usual five minutes. This is a huge improvement for him since he has doubled his performance.

However, he is still labeled ADHD, and being out of his seat is still ADHD behavior. The fact that he did better today, which should be seen and reinforced as a step in the right direction, often is not noticed. His move in the right direction is not reinforced. So, the probability of a repeat of his increased "staying in seat behavior" is reduced.

The environment must reinforce the new, more positive behaviors. No treatment makes the child impervious to further insult. The child can only continue positive behavior because of, not in spite of, his situation.

The ADHD Label Can Obscure Strengths

Chapter 21

The "H" In ADHD

To adults, one of the most irritating qualities of ADHD is the hyperactivity. It stood out enough to be one of the first labels for these children — hyperactive. Within the rubric of hyperactivity are actually six different processes that get clumped together. The common thread that connects them is not activity level but the annoyance they cause others.

ADHD as a Service to Other Children

Many other students, not labeled ADHD, share the ADHD child's same feelings about school. Their feelings are just not as strong, or they have adapted in other ways.

I remember going to an elementary school to observe Travis, a child diagnosed with ADHD. About one third of the children in the classroom were in the same emotional situation as Travis. Indeed, I could not see how my patient's behavior was any different than theirs. The whole fourth grade class seemed on the verge of being out of control.

But Travis' antics provided a distraction from work the other children also did not want to do. Although it was not Travis' choice, functionally, he was just the first to "see the potential market and provide the service." He was the entrepreneur who supplied the comic relief from the deadly serious drama of education.

It is easy for the ADHD child to make other children laugh because of the tension they also carry. In other words, he is an entertainer, expressing the frustrations of others. Then, when other children laugh and snicker in response to his performances, those laughs and snickers are experienced as reward.

For the ADHD child who does not have many genuine sources of social approval from peers, this classroom arena for his performances quickly shapes acting out behavior.

He also provides another service for his classmates. He is their cover. Since his antics are usually more intense, he draws the teacher's "fire" so that his peers' minor misconducts go unpunished. In fact, by comparison with the ADHD child, their behaviors — fidgeting, talking, etc. — do not seem too deviant.

In this way, "normal" children live in the shadow of the ADHD child. And the ADHD child and his peers exchange valuable services such that each benefits.

If each group is not provided with an alternate avenue for these rewards, the disruptive interaction pattern will be very difficult to change. If the individual ADHD child is removed from this symbiotic reinforcement exchange, another child is likely to take his place — because the basic dynamics of the situation still have not been altered.

The Self Reinforcing Quality of Hyperactivity

The ADHD child's depression may fuel the hyperactivity. Such children describe the internal sensation of "getting hyper," as they call it, as fun. It may be that self-hyping (hyperactivity) is negatively reinforced because of its antidepressant effects. (Remember, negative reinforcement is not the same as punishment. Rather, it is the pleasure that one gets when something bad stops. In this case, hyperactivity is reinforced because it feels good to have the depression stop.)

In this vein, it is interesting to note that antidepressant medications have been found useful for these children (Biderman et. al. 1990). In fact, there is an increasing trend for physicians to prescribe antidepressants (Gammon, et. al. 1993) such as Prozac, Paxil, Effexor, and Zoloft for ADHD.

In a broader sense, the hyper state is inherently pleasurable for most people. We all enjoy the stimulation we feel in our bodies and minds when we are excited about something. Sometimes it feels good to drink a couple extra cups of coffee just for the rush it provides. (The espresso craze is testimony to this.) This is why drug addicts sometimes take stimulant drugs like Methamphetamine, Dexedrine, or Ritalin.

This same principle applies to the ADHD child, but he has learned to generate internal "drugs" when he wants to get that rush. This internally controlled self-stimulation is a stark contrast to the "boring" situation he often finds himself in.

He could be admired by us for his resourcefulness — on his own, he has developed ways of insulating himself from the negative school or home experience and generating some positive feelings.

Along this line, the hyperactive state is another way of blocking negative input. Since his manic state is so output oriented, little attention is left to process input. This is similar to the idea that you can't listen when you are talking. By not "listening" to the negative feedback, ADHD children do not have to experience it.

The ADHD Child's Unresponsiveness to Other's Feelings

The ability of the ADHD child to filter out negative feedback is probably what also accounts for the adult perception that ADHD children are insensitive to the feelings and desires of others.

They are not insensitive to other's feelings in a non-caring sense. Rather, by attentional avoidance, they filter out of their consciousness the negative feedback from others. That leaves the child "flying blind" in interpersonal situations.

He thus offends more and more people, more and more often, and is less and less aware of the potentially corrective feedback. He tramples people everywhere but is systematically unaware of it.

Despite this consistent negative feedback from peers, the ADHD child is socially busy. He engages in the same amount of activity as normal children, but in counterproductive ways (Cunningham, Siegel, & Offord, 1985; Grenell, Glass, & Katz, 1987; Marsh & Johnston, 1982). His perseverance in seeking social contact makes sense when one understands that ADHD children have learned to blank out the negative parts of their reality and respond only to the positive residual of the feedback sent their way.

This is why ADHD children are able to report that they have many friends, while actually having few.

ADHD Consciousness: A Collage

Some ADHD children also describe their internal mental experience as being very disjointed, like a collage. They talk about confusion, not remembering things, not knowing why they do things, and a sudden intrusion of feelings.

This frustrating and frightening experience is caused by swinging back and forth between reality and "outer space," i.e. being spaced out. Their spaced out, attentional avoidance is not perfect, therefore, certain types of strong outside stimulus will eventually interrupt the avoidance process and force the child back into reality.

When ADHD children return to the real world, it is not where they left it. This is experienced as a sense of confusion and of missing segments from both mental states. Their remembered, disjointed, collage-like vignettes are not always translatable into a continuous, meaningful story.

This can be very disturbing, particularly as they get older and more performance demands are made on them. And, with the increased introspective ability that comes with adolescence and adulthood, many of them begin to realize that their experience of consciousness is not the same as others.

One aspect of this is the observable, sudden mood changes in the ADHD child. One minute he will be calm, the next angry, the next depressed. Sometimes adults will ask if the child is manic-depressive (bipolar). I have met some adult ADHD patients who have been diagnosed as manic-depressive and medicated accordingly.

Junkyard Dog Hyper-vigilance (Anger)

The similarities between the ADHD child and "junkyard dogs" are really quite striking. Junkyard dogs are interesting, scary, and pitiful animals. If you try to get near them, they get very agitated, bark, and run back and fourth.

The ADHD child's hyperactivity is an example of the same agitated, heightened emotional arousal. Both are angry, unhappy and aggressive toward others.

You create a junkyard dog the same way you create an ADHD child. You make a junkyard dog by restraining him with a leash then beating him regularly. When he sees you coming, in anticipation of another beating, he becomes agitated, hyper-vigilant, barks, and tries to bite you.

The path to ADHD in a child is quite similar, though the restraint and punishment we use are mostly verbal and social, rather than physical.

We verbally restrain them to their seats while we make them do aversive tasks. We verbally punish them when their performance on those aversive tasks falls below our standards. Like the junkyard dog, the ADHD child becomes hyper-vigilant and hyperactive when the potential punisher (teacher or parent) approaches.

If it is true for junkyard dogs, why wouldn't it be true for ADHD children? Why would we expect anything else? It is not our good intentions but our behavior toward these children that shapes their behavior.

Chapter 22

ADHD, Behavior Disabilities, and Learning Disabilities: Branches of the Same Tree

Now let us look at how Attention Deficit Hyperactivity Disorder, Behavior Disorder, and Learning Disability are related.

For conceptual clarity, I will discuss each of these three problems separately, in their pure forms, which seldom occurs in the real world.

Generally, children will display all of these "disorders," but they tend to capitalize on opportunities unique to their particular disorder. All three are variations on the same strategy, which is to escape noxious stimuli. ADHD children use an attentional strategy, whereas Learning Disabilities and Behavior Disabilities patients use behavioral escape routes.

How ADHD, Behavior Disabilities, & Learning Disabilities Attentionally Avoid Differently

How each "disability" reframes the aversive situation is its defining characteristic. The ADHD child attempts to both avoid conflict and avoid being thought of as stupid. He attentionally checks out of the whole scene.

Behavior Disabilities and Learning Disabilities children manipulate how the world reacts to them with behavioral strategies. The Learning Disabilities child would rather be thought dumb than deal with confrontation. The Behavior Disabilities child would rather provoke uproar and confrontation than to be thought dumb.

Which adaptation pattern develops probably depends on the child's broader learning history and current reinforcement contingencies. The following examples illustrate the difference in the style and focus of the child's attentional avoidance strategy.

Internal Attentional Strategy

Effram was a busy young man who seemed to skip like a stone across the water, never getting wet. One minute he would be working at a table with other children, the next minute he would be playing with something in his pocket, and the next minute he would be in the back room looking through the art supplies.

He seemed to have the knack of moving on to the next activity before much could go wrong with the last one. He was all output with little input.

When I would ask him how he did today, he would always say "fine" no matter what had happened. If I brought up an incident that his teacher or parent had mentioned to me, he would just do another "skip" by changing the subject. He would pull something out of his pocket or ask me what something was or why I did something. He was an expert at slipping away from whatever focus I proposed.

These deflections were not clumsy like you might expect from some "disorder." They were expertly timed so that Effram stayed just beyond reach. He was like a sparrow feeding on your lawn, who moves just out of your way, but not very far, expending minimum amount of energy.

ADHD Takes an Attentional Vacation to Fantasyland

The avoidance strategies of a particular ADHD child tend to be generalized to many academic, interpersonal, social, and situational cues. His responses are so diffused and diverse that he spends a large portion of his time moving from task to task, situation to situation, and person to person in an effort to avoid noxious stimuli.

For him, many cues, such as the classroom itself, the other children, his desk, the teacher, and so forth, are conditioned stimuli that provoke unpleasant feelings in him. The only comfortable ground is to escape into fantasy, like Nintendo. This child goes on automatic pilot when he first senses the proximity of any negative cues. This may be seen as either passive "checking out" with no apparent motor behavior, or it may manifest as behavior problems, or some combination of the two.

When such a child attentionally avoids numerous cues, he may appear continuously detached and inattentive to the environment. His adaptations are not as clearly defined as either the Behavior Disabilities or Learning Disabilities child.

External Behavioral Strategies

Behavior Disabilities Use Chaos to Distract from Being Thought Dumb

The chaos the Behavior Disabilities child generates is a decoy to distract attention away from his failings. He then avoids the threat of being thought dumb, which is less embarrassing to him than exposing his academic incompetence.

For example, he is more embarrassed by having to read a paragraph out loud in class than by the consequences of causing a classroom disruption. He also realizes that nothing really bad happens as a result of causing some uproar. The angry response distracts everyone, including the teacher, from the original intent. Therefore, his response to the teacher's (or parent's) original instructions is irrelevant after the chaos he caused.

To him, it is more important to avoid another failure experience than to take a little verbal flack for one's behavior.

Jerry was proud to announce to me that he had a "rep" with the other children in his ninth grade class. His parents and teacher reported that he was regularly disruptive in class. This happened most often when he was called upon. Instead of responding appropriately, he would wise crack, yell or cuss.

When I asked Jerry why he disrupted the class when he was called upon, he retorted, "I don't have to do that f—ing crap. I have had enough of Mr. Dawson harassing me."

When I had him return to these incidents while on CAER, he at first felt very angry at Mr. Dawson. Once this was extinguished, he began to talk about how embarrassed he felt about answering in class because one time he had said something wrong and the other kids had laughed at him.

"Mr. Dawson isn't going to trick me into letting the other kids laugh at me again," he said. "Next time I won't just beat them up, I'll beat him up too."

Jerry's manhood was at stake, and he was going to defend it any way he had to.

Performance demands — such as reading and grades — are particularly threatening to the young male ego as the adolescent struggles for his position in the pecking order of other young males.

In trying to move up the pecking order, he is faced with a sharp contrast between the outcome of different choices. There is a great deal of reinforcement for aggression within the young male social system, for strength, toughness, speed, loudness, athletic skill, and intimidation skills. But there is great embarrassment at being thought a wimp. There is a small amount of reinforcement for being intelligent. But there is great embarrassment for being thought dumb.

When you are up to your rear in alligators it is difficult to remember that your original intent was to drain the swamp

When the young male is confronted with an academic performance demand that he is not confident he can accomplish, he has two choices. He can make an effort at meeting the academic challenge. Or, he can be aggressive.

If he chooses to meet the challenge and succeeds, he may get some reinforcement. The problem with this, though, is that from his point of view, there is little probability of succeeding. And, if he fulfills his prophesy and fails, he is faced with overwhelming embarrassment.

208

On the other hand, if he is aggressive, he will be highly thought of by his peers and certainly will not be classified as a wimp. He will also have avoided the embarrassment of having appeared stupid.

The experience of anger also feels better for the young male than the embarrassment of exposing his "stupidity." Rather than experiencing the feelings of helplessness and weakness that come with academic failure, the anger brings feelings of strength, power, and control. From the Behavior Disabilities child's point of view, the choice is clear, act out.

Tracing the Behavior Disabilities child's experience of a threatening event, especially if it has caused disruption, is also informative. For example, the Behavior Disabilities child might sense the coming frustration of doing a math assignment when the teacher begins to pass out worksheets. As soon as the papers are passed to him, he feels a subtle sense of discomfort. He tries to avoid this discomfort, and resulting feeling of failure, by emitting distracting behavior.

He might do this by changing his perception of the math handouts from something dreaded to something more pleasant. He might imagine the assignment sheets as toys and throw the papers like a ball to the next student. When this happens, the meaning of the papers and the related situation is transformed. The failure feeling produced by math assignments is transformed into an object of play, something to throw to another student. And that feels much, much better.

From the child's point of view, this is a clever, skillful, adaptive strategy. Class uproar and scolding by the teacher is better than feeling anxious or dumb. It is important to see the Behavior Disabilities child's behavior as self-preserving, skilled, and effective.

It is a myth that these acting out behaviors occur because "He can't control himself." He quite effectively controls himself, the teacher, the other children in the class, the vice- principal, and his parents, just not in the way we want.

Learning Disabilities Use Dumb to Avoid Conflict

The first time I saw Brad, I got sucked in all the way. He seemed like the perfect child therapy patient. He wanted to tell me about how bad he was doing in reading and how awful it made him feel. Each time I saw him he told me more about how hard he tried, how much work he did, and how much he liked his teacher.

I too worked hard to help Brad, but nothing I did seemed to make any difference. Still, his parents were pleased because he looked forward to seeing me each week — I had "such a good relationship with him."

The clue to what was happening occurred when I found that he had few friends his own age and his teacher, counselor, and reading tutor were all in the same predicament with him that I was. We were all working too hard, making no progress, and he seemed to be enjoying every bit of it. He had discovered how to hook each one of us into giving him a great deal of undivided attention, which he preferred to peer attention.

The story changed dramatically when we changed the rules for adult attention. We all made our time with him contingent on his successful performance, rather than his frustration and failures. He could no longer come to us to tell us his hard luck stories. He had to read better, behave better, and be happier to spend time with me. His parents would make an appointment for him with me when he could come show me some evidence of his improvement. This might be a good spelling test or a story about having spent a good day at a friend's house.

This coordinated effort by all of his adult helpers to change the rules in his life dramatically improved his mood and performance.

The "pure" Learning Disabilities (LD) child's approach is the opposite of the Behavior Disabilities child. He is quieter and more socially endearing. So, while he may fail at a task, his behavior does not elicit the angry, negative feedback that is evoked by his overly active and abrasive counterparts.

In fact, the LD child is willing to own and absorb the problem as his personal academic defect, rather than suffer disapproval for his behavior. His compliant demeanor combines with his academic failing to garner help and caring from adults. But the adults very efforts to help can be one of the child's reinforcers for LD. That's because the LD child yearns for this one-on-one adult attention.

Usually, the LD child's avoidance is focused on a particular academic task or subject. This task, be it math, reading, or social studies, arouses strong emotional responses in the child.

For example, he might take the math worksheets and begin to work diligently until faced with a difficult problem. Some preconditioned cue in the difficult problem, be it the quantity of numbers, or maybe the operator [+,-,x.,/], ignites the failure feelings.

When this happens, the LD child becomes so anxious that he cognitively blanks out the material to be learned, like stage fright or blanking out on an exam, and internal dialogues of failure take over his mind. The child's learning abilities are overwhelmed by his anxious state.

Indeed, LD children become so anxious, worried, and depressed when they are confronted with a learning task that there is little cognitive ability left for learning or retrieval of information.

Emotional blocking of intellectual abilities has long been noted on intellectual tests such as the Wechsler intelligence tests (Kaufman, 1979). When children are emotionally stressed, performance drops on sub-tests that require sustained attention.

Soon he becomes so intellectually inefficient he learns little and appears to be learning disabled on LD tests. In essence, though, the child has a circumscribed phobia of a specific academic task. Since he blames himself for his failing, depression is often also part of the picture.

When these children are desensitized in therapy to the academic situation — task, teacher, schoolmates, etc.— their grades usually rise systematically. Many children make sudden dramatic improvements.

For example, a high school junior with a long history of poor academic performance was failing German. In the week after CAER was used to desensitize his fear of learning German, a national standardized German test was given. He received the highest grade in the school. Both he and his teacher were startled.

CAER did not teach him any new German, but his anxiety was reduced so that he could access the German he had been learning all along.

The procedure was repeated with the rest of his subjects. He subsequently earned some of the top grades in his class in several other courses.

How ADHD, Learning Disabilities and Behavior Disabilities Fit Together in Real Life

From the child's perspective, all three disorders are doing the same thing, avoiding experiencing bad feelings. Therefore, in real life, pure examples are seen rarely. Most children combine all three strategies.

(For simplicity of discussion of ADHD, Learning Disabilities, and Behavior Disabilities problems, the larger scope of emotional problems, neurological variations, and academic learning history brought with the child into the school system are not discussed here.

These factors may contribute to some ADHD, Behavior Disabilities, and Learning Disabilities problems, but, in my estimation, they do not account for the majority of the problems.)

Academic Survival

The Academic Consequences of ADHD and Behavior Disabilities

Because the behavioral disruption of the ADHD child often takes precedence over his learning problems, he is treated like the Behavior Disabilities child. In order not to provoke the Behavior Disabilities child, he is often placed in a special classroom that provides more individual attention, more structure, more tolerance for acting out, and fewer academic demands. Such an approach naturally flows from the traditional conceptualization of Behavior Disabilities.

This tends to lead to better academic progress and fewer behavior problems. It also leads to less experience and skill in dealing with actual real world demands. Therefore, the reduced demands of these special classrooms often act inadvertently as a reward for the child's previous acting out.

Because of this, many of these children are quite articulate about not wanting to return to regular classrooms.

The Academic Consequences of Learning Disabilities

The school system is yoked with the task of adapting to the Learning Disabilities child's learning style. Special teaching techniques are offered that the child may find easier. Such approaches are predicated on the idea that the Learning Disabilities child's learning or sensory modality is defective, at least when compared to that which is culturally dominant.

Teachers and counselors will say that the child is "auditory" or "kinesthetic" in learning style, not visually oriented, which is the culturally dominant style. So, they say, a different way of inputting information must be used.

I have seen high-level school personnel argue this point with reference to a child who regularly demonstrates outstanding drawing skills. This child could not be a good artist if he did not have good visualization skills, in fact better than most.

For the vast majority of the children labeled as either auditory or kinesthetic, it is likely that the therapeutic effect of using an alternate teaching strategy is the result of the Nintendo effect — there is no negative learning history with them. They are simply using procedures and materials that are novel to the child. Like Nintendo, he attends to them, at least until they become conditioned with an aversive emotional tone.

It is, in all probability, this lack of negative learning history that makes these alternate teaching strategies work, not the sensory modality they supposedly represent.

Adults with ADHD

ADHD can be a pervasive, life-long problem extending into adulthood. Not only can it destroy academic performance and self- esteem, it can also impact future success as an adult.

Overall, the way adults with ADHD describe their experiences is congruent with children's descriptions. They talk about jumpy feelings, spacing out, "finding" themselves doing things, having a poor self concept, denying failure and rejection, and enjoying being hyped up.

They tend to express appreciation and relief when finally someone understands what their experience is like, particularly if something can be done to solve their problem.

Treatment with adult ADHD patients proceeds much as it does with children, except that their lives have accumulated many more scars. These scars often have to be treated in their own right.

Tim, 29 Years Old and Learning Disabled

Tim came to treatment at age 29. A high school graduate, who could read no more than his name and simple street signs, Tim had been in numerous special education classes through elementary school but could not learn to read.

During high school he hung out in shop classes. He was generally tolerated because he did not cause major problems, though he would occasionally use a few expletives on teachers who would try to force him to read out loud in class.

His learning problem centered around reading. It was apparent from his general language ability that he had at least normal intelligence.

Tim was consistently employed in the same skilled manufacturing job for 13 years. He felt that his upward mobility in that company or elsewhere was severely hampered by his inability to read.

His treatment was also complicated because his wife was in the process of leaving him and filing for a divorce. He had decided that it was time to do something with his life.

Tim's description of his emotional life was congruent with his rebellious appearance, long hair down to the middle of his back and a fu man chu beard. He had a long history of angry outbursts going back to early childhood. Much of this was directed at teachers and peers. His marriage was also an angry relationship. CAER treatment focused on Tim's anger.

Current or recent angry experiences were identified, the affect experienced, then traced back across his life. This procedure was repeated innumerable times. He seemed to have an endless supply of angry and frustrating experiences to extinguish.

A volunteer reading tutor was also engaged for weekly help in reading skill development. His reading skills began to develop immediately, and by his fifth week he was spontaneously reading subtitles on foreign movies (something that I still find difficult). By this point he was a functional reader who actively sought out things to read, including books. He described this experience as his "brain was starting to work."

With the same CAER procedure, work continued on extinguishing his still substantial but lessening supply of angry memories. Over a period of eleven one-hour treatment sessions on CAER, his angry demeanor and self-reported anger mellowed.

Chapter 23

Looking Where the Light is: Kids and Medicine

Our ability to understand has always been limited by the development of our senses and our concepts. When Galileo developed the telescope, we began to explore the heavens. With the linear accelerator came the understanding of sub-atomic physics. With biochemistry came modern medicine.

Medicine's germ theory in turn has been the conceptual marvel that has led to the eradication of many infectious diseases. Medicine has fascinated us with its high technology, great advances, big bucks, and high status people. The medical model has been so successful that it has prevented a search for answers in other areas. This may be illustrated by the following story.

The Story of the Lost Keys

One man is walking down the street at night. He comes upon a second man who is on his knees under a street light digging in the gutter.

The first man asks, "What are you doing?"

The second man answers, "Looking for my keys."

The first man asks, "Can I help?"

The second man answers, "Sure, thanks."

The first asks, "Where did you lose your keys?"

The second man replies, "Over there," and he points into the darkness.

The first asks, "Then why are you looking here?"

The second man replies, "Because this is where the light is."

Because of the demonstrated power of the medical model, medicine has an aura of being closer to the light of the truth, no matter where the keys to the problem were lost.

Within this metaphor, the ADHD child is in the light provided by the language of the medical model. It is difficult to walk out of a light that has been so productive. Nevertheless, it is time to do so.

Our understanding of our intellectual and physical process has been organized around medical concepts. We have Mental Health Centers rather than Philosophy Nooks or Thought Barns. Initially cutting edge ideas like the medical model are a vehicle for increased progress. But as the models age, they inhibit the adoption of the next innovative model.

Current solutions for ADHD are not working because they are not searching where the keys were lost. The new territory is illuminated by psychological learning theory, which provides clear direction in resolving ADHD.

Advantages of the Conditioned Attentional Avoidance Loop Model

In contrast to the medical model, the advantage of the Conditioned Attentional Avoidance Loop Model is that it points a way to treatment that directly alleviates the problem rather than controls it.

The neurological hypotheses that are currently popular offer the patient little hope other than stimulant medication and behavior modification. Both of these approaches are directed at controlling ADHD but offer nothing toward correcting the core attentional problem.

The Conditioned Attentional Avoidance Loop Model, on the other hand, offers the probability of cure, as opposed to life-long management.

Computer Aided Emotional Restructuring is one treatment that provides the cure.

Chapter 24

Computer Aided Emotional Restructuring: How it Works

History

Computer Aided Emotional Restructuring (CAER) was not invented out of a vacuum. The theory behind it springs from Eye Movement Desensitization and Reprocessing (EMD/R), first brought to the attention of the psychological community by Francine Shapiro (1989a, 1989b). EMD/R is a powerful, and increasingly popular, new psychotherapeutic technique.

But long before Shapiro's discovery, others (Headstrom, 1991) noted that eye movement patterns have long been prescribed in the yoga literature for relaxation and concentration.

EMD/R is described by Shapiro (1989a, p. 205) as follows:

> "Subjects... were instructed to visualize the traumatic scene, rehearse the negative state- ment (e.g., 'I am helpless'), and follow the

investigator's index finger with their eyes. The investigator then caused subjects to generate a series of 10-20 voluntary, bilateral, rhythmic saccadic eye movements by moving her index finger rapidly back and forth across their line of vision. The finger was located 12-14 inches from the face and was moved from the extreme right to the extreme left of the visual field at a rate of two back-and-forth sweeps per second."

Since 1989, hundreds of case studies of successful treatment using EMD/R have been reported (Shapiro, 1989a, 1989b; Marquis, 1991; Wolpe & Abrams, 1991; Puk, 1991). Marquis (1991, p. 188) notes:

"The range of problems treated successfully is astonishingly broad: depression, post-traumatic stress disorder, social anxiety, disturbing dreams resulting from childhood sexual abuse, intrusive images and thoughts, flashbacks, sleep disturbances, traumatic memories concerning the Vietnam War, childhood sexual molestation, sexual or physical assault, emotional abuse, sleep disturbances, low self-esteem, headaches, learning disabilities, and relationship problems."

Evolution from EMD/R to Computer-Aided Emotional Restructuring

In 1991, Dr. Mary Weathers and I began to try EMD/R with our patients. The results were impressive. It was clear, however, given our limited physical ability to continually sweep our fingers back and forth in front of the patient eyes, that an automated means of timing the patient's eye movement would be useful.

This was the impetus for the development of the first CAER machine, which uses moving lights rather than moving fingers. Indeed, a therapist can reliably and repeatedly only do about 30 sweeps before his arm tires and fails. Thirty sweeps just begins to generate the therapeutic state.

On CAER, the typical patient can do 1,000 to 2,000 sweeps per one-hour session. The increased number of sweeps considerably strengthens the relaxed state, up to about 1,500 sweeps. However, in experiments with multi-hour sessions, up to 7,000 sweeps have been successfully used.

The addition of sound moving in synchrony with the sweeping lights, as well as the reduction of distracting stimuli, also enhances the CAER state.

How CAER Works

The active ingredients in CAER and EMD/R are not new. There seem to be three major elements of the CAER experience:

1) Deep relaxation,

2) Vivid imagery,

3) Juxtaposition of these two processes to extinguish the feelings produced by the images.

Functionally, it resembles systematic desensitization (Wolpe, 1973), but it works much more rapidly. Systematic desensitization is one of the best researched and most effective psychotherapy techniques ever developed, though it is seldom used. Why is it not used if it is so great?

Let me explain the procedure because that answers both why it works so well and why it is seldom used. Systematic desensitization is a long, drawn out process.

First, you spend five to 10 sessions teaching Jacobson deep muscle relaxation so that the patient can relax himself profoundly and on cue from the therapist.

Once this is accomplished, the therapist and patient work several more sessions to develop a progressive hierarchy of increasingly more distressing images. For example, if the patient is elevator phobic, they work out a list of images that have to do with elevators that are increasingly more anxiety-producing for the patient.

The hierarchy might start out with thinking about riding in a elevator and then include steps like seeing a building that has an elevator, walking into a building that has an elevator, seeing the elevator, walking toward the elevator, standing in front of the elevator, pressing the elevator button, seeing the doors of the elevator open, etc. Each of these steps to riding an elevator is individualized to the specific patient.

Once the relaxation is taught and the hierarchy is developed, then the real therapy begins. This may be eight to twelve sessions into the process. Are you beginning to get an idea why this therapy is seldom used?

The actual therapy consists of first having the patient use the self-relaxation techniques that have been taught. Once they are very relaxed, the therapist has the patient imagine the least threatening image. If that image makes the patient anxious, he is asked to terminate the image and relax himself. If the image does not elicit any anxiety, the patient is asked to imagine the next image and so on.

This process of alternating potentially anxiety-producing images and deep relaxation is continued until all of the images in the hierarchy can be imagined without the patient experiencing any anxiety. The technique is often continued into the real world with the patient and therapist physically retracing the steps in the hierarchy previously desensitized in the office, e.g., in the real elevator.

They continue the process until neither the image nor the in vivo experience of the elevator produces any anxiety. The patient can then ride elevators without any anxiety response. This may take far more treatment sessions than most patients are willing to do or insurance companies are willing to pay for. But if you persevere, it works well.

CAER works in a similar way to systematic desensitization, but far more quickly. The CAER machine triggers a physiological response that puts most people in a profoundly relaxed, almost sleep-like state. For most people this happens within three to ten minutes of their very first experience with CAER.

In this deeply relaxed state, their imagery is also enhanced, much as if they were dreaming. They can vividly relive emotionally distressing experiences. The powerful relaxation, just as in systematic desensitization, overpowers the anxiety and eventually extinguishes it. The image is left, willfully accessible, but no longer elicits an emotional response. In other words, the person can then think of the previously emotionally arousing event without being emotionally aroused.

The patient is aided in this because of a process that naturally occurs in the brain. The brain orders emotionally similar images into chains that serve the same function as the hierarchy of images used in systematic desensitization.

Because of this, once the patient experiences a particular feeling state, other experiences with the same feeling tone are stimulated and thereby become accessible to the patient, one after the other. Though it combines the same active elements as systematic desensitization, the process of CAER works much more quickly.

What CAER Looks Like

The technology for CAER has evolved through at least five generations of prototype models. The current version is a seven-foot long, five-foot high, three-foot wide, white fiberglass pod. It looks like a giant Easter egg laying on its side. The door on the side opens like a car door.

Inside is a foam bed with walls that are covered with soundproof foam. In the ceiling, above the patient's eyes, are two small red LED's (electronic lights). They are placed about 2.5 feet in front of the patient and horizontally about 2.5 feet apart. There is a back projection screen between the lights for displaying images, and the patient wears soundproof headphones to listen to music or other verbal stimulus.

There are also a variety of physiological sensors that are used to monitor indicators of the patient's psychological arousal.

CAER

The patient lies in the soundproof pod, with the door closed, in total darkness. The lights and sounds oscillate back and forth at about one round-trip per second. The patient watches the lights by moving his eyes back and forth in time with the moving lights and music.

Different types of music are used to elicit different emotions. The sound system can also be used to play audio tapes specifically designed to elicit and eliminate emotions.

Provocative and soothing images are displayed between the lights, depending on the therapy objective.

The Experience of CAER Treatment

For the first few moments, most people find their attention is primarily occupied by watching the lights and listening to the music. Soon this becomes automatic and effortless. While still fully conscious, the patient experiences a relaxing, alert, dreamlike state. Respiration, pulse, and Galvanic Skin Response drop to sleep-like levels. Most patients enjoy the experience of CAER. It is very relaxing, much like sleep.

When the patient thinks about negative, emotionally loaded events, first they experience the emotions attached to that image. That is, they feel like they normally do when they think about such things. After a while, the factual memory sharpens while the emotional response to the imagery weakens and eventually vanishes. This may take 15 minutes to several sessions, depending on a multitude of factors.

Concerns that formerly elicited strong emotional responses become boring and effortful to remember. In other words, the event becomes an emotionless memory that no longer drives current feelings, behaviors, and perceptions. This is what is meant by emotional extinction and is the basis of what makes CAER so effective.

The most closely related natural state to CAER therapy is the lucid dream (LaBerge, 1985) in which the person is conscious that he is dreaming while he is dreaming.

Following therapy, similar day-to-day events invoke less emotional response because they no longer have ties to similar, past, real life events.

Most children like the experience so much that they look forward to their next session. They quickly recognize that CAER therapy makes them feel better, first while in the pod and later in the real world. Children use words like "cool," "wow," and "that's something'" to describe their CAER experience. But toward the end of therapy, they do get bored (in the adult sense of the word) because, after the negative feelings are extinguished, nothing much happens.

Therapeutic Process of CAER

Most things in life go by unnoticed. As you drive down the road, most of what passes stirs no response in you. Only a few things are significant enough to create a reaction, and that is how it should be. Only things that have significance to you, based on your past experience with them, can elicit an emotional response.

Some of these responses are positive and some are negative. For instance, you may drool at the red Porsche and be frightened by the barking dog. Each is a distinct and different emotional impression that may range from joy to fear, pride to shame, gratefulness to anger, relief to hurt, comfort to loneliness, or laughter to depression.

Indeed, it is not what happens to you in life that "makes you crazy." It is how you feel about what happens to you that "makes you crazy." You cannot change what has happened to you, but you can change how you feel about those events. And that is all that counts. You can rewrite your own history, in the emotional sense.

You can do that by erasing the negative emotional loading from memories of past experiences. Images that are emotionally loaded automatically attract attention. But images that have no emotional loading, by contrast, are difficult to notice. Think about how hard it is to concentrate on a calculus textbook and how you can't stop reading a sexy novel.

Only through the power of willful attention can we force ourselves to read a calculus textbook and do the required homework. That's because the calculus textbook has no emotional loading for most of us.

A sexy novel, however, seems to suck you into its pages. That's because the words create images that trigger positive feelings. These emotionally laden images have the power to control our behavior in that we can't stop reading.

Emotions rooted in historical experiences also have the same power to control our current behavior. Without the ability of these historical learning experiences to elicit emotions, they have no power over our current feelings and behavior.

Extinguish the power of these images to evoke feelings and you erase their power to continue to twist our lives. This is exactly what CAER does. The full-color, emotional movie becomes a silent, black and white documentary of the facts of our history.

This is exactly what is supposed to happen. The memories are not lost, just the destructive feelings attached to them. These memories can be brought up willfully, but they no longer have the power to intrude into our current lives.

CAER is paradoxical. It is paradoxical because, during treatment, the therapist tries to evoke in the patient the very problems that he wishes to eliminate.

And the therapist works from the hypothesis that the patient really has most of the skills, attitudes, and beliefs that he needs to cope with his problems. But in some situations, the patient's ability to access those skills, attitudes and beliefs is inhibited by emotions.

The goal, then, is to remove the emotional barrier to accessing already present skills, rather than teaching new skills.

Auditory, visual, and physical stimuli are used, as part of CAER treatment, to provoke the experience that caused the emotional barriers. These stimuli might include particular types of music; upsetting statements by family members or teachers, which are recorded and replayed; visual images of homework, parents, or teachers; recall of disturbing memories; physical stimuli or movement to evoke pain and discomfort; and so forth.

Experiencing these upsetting emotions while on CAER subjects these feelings to the powerful extinction produced by CAER.

For example, the children may be instructed to think about math or social studies class. Initially they usually find such imagery makes them anxious and angry. In a few minutes to an hour, these feelings fade out.

In the case of the ADHD child, other people in the feedback loop, such as parents and siblings, are asked to record an audio tape. On this tape, they make statements that precede and provoke the child's problem behaviors. Statements like:

> "Don't hit your sister."
> "Be quiet."
> "If I have told you once, I have told you a million times to...."
> "Sit down and do your work."
> "Why are you always...?"
> "Is your homework done?"

Such statements serve to irritate, agitate, anger, or depress the child, even though they may not affect others in the same way.

Each of these tapes is then played to the child while he is in the CAER machine. The emotionally provocative quality of the tapes is immediately apparent. The children grimace, grunt, cuss, double up their fists, wiggle, complain, or yell while listening — an exhibition of the same emotional responses that are precursors to the child's problem behaviors.

This happens for the first few cycles through the tapes. As the tapes continue to play, over and over, the emotional arousal fades to deep relaxation. The child becomes very relaxed and eventually bored with these formerly provocative statements.

Teachers are also asked to make a tape of the things they say that precedes the child's attentional avoidance or acting out. These are typically phrases such as:

"Keep your hands to yourself."
"Do your math now."
"Sit down and stop talking."
"It is time for your spelling."

Though they may be obviously irritating statements, they need not be. In reality, the statements have simply become a signal to the ADHD child that something he does not like is coming, such as a math assignment.

After listening to the teachers' and parents' tapes, the words lose their emotional impact and become only words — words unadorned by conditioned emotional responses. And the words lose their learned power to evoke emotions. Because of this, children's behavior and academic performance tends to improve markedly.

Also, as the powerful negative emotions fade, behavior and feelings that are normally suppressed emerge. And the child can access skills, strengths, and abilities that previously had not been at his disposal.

When the children return to class, the angry and anxious feelings are no longer stimulated. Typically, their performance improves because it is easier to concentrate on the material and they have better access to the skills they already have.

Chapter 25

Therapeutic Effects of CAER

What Makes Emotional Extinction so Effective

As stated before, most people function less than optimally because historical emotional learning confounds their perception of current situations. In essence, one distorts current emotions and perceptions to seem more like their historical emotional roots. It is as though there is an emotional blending or fusion of the historical with the current. This means that our responses, emotionally and behaviorally, are not responding truly to the current situation and therefore may be ineffective.

One can see this in the example of a husband who is angry at his wife when she makes a simple request of him. He does not really hear the request, as she states it, because of his conditioned learning history with "women making requests."

Rather, he feels and responds the way he did to his controlling mother. As such, he often creates a problem with his wife where there is none because he had a problem with his mother.

Current situations press on old bruises and thus are more upsetting than they should be. By healing those bruises from the past, the present is experienced as a mellower, less distressing reality.

For the ADHD child, the current math assignment seems worse than it really is because it reminds him of the bad feelings he experienced from previous math assignments. Extinguishing these old feelings allows the child to respond to the current assignment for what it really is, rather than what it reminds him of.

Traditional psychotherapy attempts to do this by allowing the patient to repeatedly re-experience these historically upsetting events in a safe, comfortable setting. CAER functions in a similar manner, only much more quickly.

Some might wonder if the emotional extinction leads people to be overly bland. Yes, patients do become unemotional in that they no longer respond to certain stimuli. But, this unemotional reaction applies only to those cues that previously set off negative emotional responses. There is no overall flattening affect.

Actually, the happy, positive side of the personality seems to be more apparent after CAER treatment. This is probably because the generalized inhibition that was previously used to attempt to control the negative emotional responses is no longer necessary. So, both children and adults seem, not only less troubled, but also generally more joyful and relaxed.

CAER is a Non-aggressive Method for Dealing with the Anger

One of the most powerful and destructive emotions that intrude into our lives is anger. Suppression of anger causes a variety of physical and psychological pathologies. Expressing it causes negative social repercussions, which is a double bind.

But how to deal with anger besides suppressing or expressing it has been a mystery.

CAER provides an alternative disposition for anger that causes neither social, psychological, nor physical pathologies. The anger is eliminated without directing it inward or outward.

The angry emotions are just extinguished.

Cognitive Behavior Therapy and CAER

Cognitive Behavior Therapy is a popular treatment methodology that deserves some mention both because research supports its effectiveness for some problems and because it has some relevance to CAER.

Cognitive Behavior Therapy is based on the premise that people's subconscious speech and thoughts can cause emotional problems because these speech and thoughts are often illogical and dysfunctional. There is no doubt that this is true.

From our personal experience, we all know that we can depress ourselves if we go around telling ourselves how stupid we are, how awful the world is, how hopeless our situation is, how no one loves or cares about us. Those words have emotional responses conditioned to them, which one experiences as depression.

In Cognitive Behavior Therapy, the therapist first tries to identify the individual patient's unique dysfunctional thoughts. His strategy is to eliminate the thoughts, thereby eliminating the bad feelings they cause.

He works to stop these dysfunctional thoughts by logically persuading the patient that these emotionally upsetting thoughts are illogical and without substantive basis. Patients are also taught to use the same logical technique to refute their own illogical thought patterns. This process immediately tends to interrupt these unhappy thoughts.

Cognitive Behavior Therapy was initially thought to be useful for ADHD patients, but recent research does not demonstrate long-term effectiveness (Abikoff, 1991).

CAER Uses Extinction vs. Cognitive Persuasion

CAER addresses these same dysfunctional thought patterns, but from a different perspective. CAER changes repetitive, negative thought patterns through an elimination process rather than cognitive persuasion. Instead of the mental isometrics required to oppose the distress-causing thought with a second refuting thought, CAER uses extinction of the emotions triggered by the thoughts.

There turns out to be a two-way relationship between words that create bad feelings and the bad feelings that produce those words. That is, bad feelings beget bad words and bad words beget bad feelings. The loop can be started or broken on the word side or on the feeling side. If you extinguish either or both sides of this thought loop, mood improves.

One can approach this CAER extinction process from either the word or the feeling side. If one starts from the feeling side, young children are asked to relive current bad feelings by "thinking about things that bug them or make them mad."

Older children are asked to think about what it feels like to be in a particular situation that creates anxiety for them — such as reading in class, taking a spelling test, getting reprimanded, being in math class or doing homework.

Once they find that place, then they are asked to be like a bloodhound. The therapist will say, for example, "You know how you give a bloodhound someone's sock, and he sniffs it. Then he trots off, following the scent and finds the owner. Well, that is what I want you to do with the feeling you get in math class (when someone makes you mad). Once you can really feel what it's like to be in math class, I want you to find all the other places that give you the same feeling." (Watkins, 1978)

As they follow the emotional thread, the learning history unfolds. Logical understanding of problems tends to arise spontaneously as sudden insight, secondary to the emotional extinction, and requires no effort from the patient.

Being an Emotional Bloodhound

The ADHD child will spontaneously describe how learning subtraction in second grade felt the same way as doing current fifth grade math homework. Subtraction in second grade is connected by a feeling thread to fifth grade math homework. The emotional experience of any current situation or stimuli is the summation of the connecting emotional links to historical experience.

As the child travels back and forth across the negative feelings, over time, the feelings that are extinguished become progressively more difficult to follow. Eventually the thread becomes so faint that their mind wanders off to other things.

Present experiences that were connected by the thread are freed from their emotional links to the past and thereby stand on their own as just current experiences. Current experience, without the negative emotional conditioning from the past, becomes less aversive.

One bad feeling after another is identified and traced back over the child's life. The child is instructed to think or do whatever they can to make the bad feeling worse. For example, the child might be asked to think of the other things that make him mad. Eventually, all the negative feelings are eliminated.

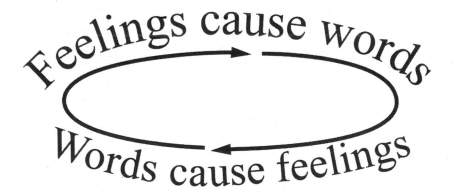

One can also approach this word-feeling loop from the word side. This may mean asking the ADHD child to call himself names or berate himself with such phrases as "I am dumb," "No one likes me," "I can't do anything right."

These are only the things he normally does with diligence, over and over. But after saying such phrases with CAER, the words change from distressing to boring, i.e. they lose their power to provoke negative emotions. This works whether the thoughts are framed as words or feelings. The patient eventually responds to them like a boring calculus text — his mind wanders.

Most children then stop thinking these self-defeating thoughts in real life and their unhappiness lifts. We talk about the children as having built a better self-image or improved self-esteem. Actually, self-esteem was there all the time. It did not have to be built. The child just had to stop poisoning it.

Behaviors are not the problem but are just the manifestation of these emotional links. Behaviors are just ways of resolving the feelings that precede them. Treatment directed at the emotional energy behind behaviors can make dramatic changes in both the emotions and their behavioral aftermath. The connecting emotional threads are the engine, and extinguishing these threads with CAER leaves the offending behaviors with no emotion to resolve.

I jokingly tell my adult patients that I have the world's best job. All day long I get to tell people to "go to hell" — their own personal hell. Then I get to hold their feet to the fires of their hell until they stop wiggling. And to think, I get paid to do this!

Matt – An 11-Year-Old ADHD's Experience With CAER

While on CAER and reviewing his ADHD experiences in class, 11-year-old Matt spontaneously described his "spacing out in class" as "it feels like being pulled into a black hole ... feels good ... escape from the bad math assignment feeling." The "bad, bad math assignment feeling" was described as a unique "yetchie feeling in [his] stomach."

He traced these feelings to the age of six, when he was in first grade. It went with the situational demand "to have to learn stuff." It was particularly associated with first grade math. In second grade, it was associated with classroom exercises using "cups of beans for subtraction"

This procedure was confusing for him in that he felt that they had "somehow switched (the) rules" on how he had understood the method of subtraction. In third grade the stomach feeling was associated with his first exposure to cursive writing, multiplication, and division.

During Matt's initial exposure to each of these memories using CAER, he felt the pull into the black hole and the "yetchie" feeling in his stomach. After sinking into these memories and feelings for a few minutes, the pull went away as did the feeling in his stomach.

After extinguishing these physiological and emotional responses to these school stimuli, he was able to focus all of his intellectual energy on the academic tasks at hand, rather than distributing his cognitive energy across both emotional and intellectual tasks.

He was more focused and efficient in the use of his mental resources. In real life, this quickly translated into the best grades ever, less anxiety, and better peer relationships.

His mother, herself a schoolteacher, was very appreciative of his new homework style. She had been accustomed to spending hours with him every night doing his homework with him. After two sessions of CAER, he did his homework thoroughly, willingly, and by himself. He was no longer locked into an emotional struggle with his mother over his homework. Prompting or cajoling was no longer necessary. She would just check his homework for completeness and accuracy before he was allowed to play.

It is interesting to note that before doing CAER with Matt, both he and his mother had been repeatedly and in detail instructed to do homework in this new manner, that is with minimal intervention on the part of mother. Though she understood the benefits of such a strategy, she was unable to implement it until the emotional connections driving this enmeshed homework behavior were extinguished in her with CAER.

After the CAER treatment, this new and more productive approach to homework seemed obvious, natural, and easy. It took emotional change, not intellectual understanding, to make the obvious changes in this homework pattern.

Matt, like most children following CAER treatment, found that schoolwork and homework caused little emotional arousal at all. It was just something that had to be done. That does not mean that children like Matt now delight in schoolwork. A truly positive experience in school depends on its inherent characteristics, like the quality of teaching.

Some children, with increasing success at school actually begin to view it as a rewarding and positive experience. As ADHD children begin to feel competent, they also learn to value the experience. We all tend to like what we are good at.

Chapter 26

The Family System and CAER

The Stages of Treatment

The treatment of ADHD children and their families goes through three stages:

1) Extinguishing the child's ADHD attentional and emotional patterns,

2) Extinguishing the negative interaction patterns between family members, and finally.

3) Contingency management.

The first step, which is what the discussion so far has focused on, is to use CAER to extinguish the child's ADHD attentional and emotional patterns.

Then, in the second step, the whole family system must be involved in treatment. ADHD is a family problem, not just the child's problem. Its roots reach back in time to before the child was born. And these roots must be dealt with as part of the therapy process so that the child does not get pulled back into the problematic family induction patterns.

Some family problems must be treated separate from, and as antedating, the ADHD child. Many parents will have to be involved in their own individual CAER therapy to deal with the personal issues that they brought to the marriage.

Once this is well under way, the final third step can begin, the contingency management stage. This involves setting up rules, contracts, point systems, and the like to make sure the new, more positive behavior patterns are reinforced. Sometimes near the end of therapy, traditional talk therapy or teaching is sometimes useful.

Parents Baggage ... Carrying It to the Next Generation

Some experts have hypothesized that because about 25 percent of ADHD children have a parent with ADHD, this means that it is genetically transmitted. This is too simplistic an explanation. Many patterns are passed on through modeling and other forms of learning. We tend to have the same political biases, language, speech patterns, values, religion, walk, and gestures as our parents. It is unlikely that these similarities are all genetically driven.

No one would dare suggest that being Catholic, speaking English, or being a Democrat is genetically determined. And these are far more complex learned behaviors than ADHD, Behavior Disabilities or Learning Disabilities. We are the most powerful learning machines on the planet.

Indeed, it is generally accepted that parents subtly teach their children emotional patterns and learned behavioral patterns. The mechanisms that transmit those patterns from generation to generation are the exact same mechanisms used to transmit ADHD behavior from one generation to another.

Briefly, parents and children develop a "dance" of compatible roles. These roles serve as a structure for learning and replicating complex behaviors, with their own patterns of reinforcement between parent and child (Bandura, 1962). Therefore, the adults have preconditioned the situation to respond to these behavior patterns. And when the child acts out the same behaviors, the environment is prepared and reinforces them.

This dance can be extremely complex and life encompassing. For example, dad may get angry often and yell at his son. His son cowers and runs off when dad yells. Dad is negatively reinforced for yelling because the son that irritates him goes away. His son's running away is negatively reinforced because it gets him away from his yelling father.

This exchange becomes habitual and we think of it as roles. If dad is angry with one family member, he is likely angry with others, so other family members have also learned to cower and run off. His son has learned more than just running away, he has watched other family members run away and he has watched how his father gets angry.

As he grows older, he begins to try out some of dad's angry behaviors. Because the family has learned to run from one angry male, he finds that some family members will run away from him, just like they run from dad. He is now being negatively reinforced for the display of anger just like dad was. Has the son inherited an angry trait?

It is easier to explain the angry son's behavior as learned than to postulate some genetic transmission. This same type of learning pattern can account for a wide range of subtle and complex behaviors and feelings including the transmission of ADHD from generation to generation.

Wayne and His Family's Experience With CAER

Wayne was a 16 year recalcitrant adolescent with ADHD. He was constantly punching holes in the walls of his room, slamming doors, confronting his mother. He said he hated his father, a truck driver who was seldom home. When dad came home everything straightened out for the few days he was home because dad was angry, grouchy and occasionally violent. Everyone walked on eggs to avoid provoking dad's anger, but that was really impossible. Dad always found some reason to growl at the family. No one messed with Wayne when dad was away. No one messed with dad when he was home.

For the first three sessions of CAER we focused on Wayne's anger at school, dad, sister, mother and just about every thing else in his life. His behavior began to improve at home and school.

I did not meet dad until the fourth session, the first time he was in town. Though he was angry, he was not the ogre that I had expected. He was very concerned about his son and family in general. He realized that he was often too angry at them, but did not know what to do about it. He often linked trips closely so that he would not be home more than overnight. He felt that this would prevent his disrupting his family. He was empathetic with his son's struggle for he had dropped out of high school because of similar problems. He would likely have been labeled ADHD if such diagnoses had existed when he was in school.

At this fourth session mother was not the take charge person I had come to know. She was quiet, anxious and somewhat cutting. They also reported that Wayne had had several angry outbursts in the six days dad had been home. Clearly, dad's presence changed family behavior, and he knew it. Because he could see the changes that CAER treatment had already made in his son he agreed to participate in CAER treatment himself. Since he was gone so much of the time, we scheduled several multi-hour sessions each time he was in town.

Though treatment primarily focused on father and son, mother participated in three sessions of CAER to extinguish some of her own hyper-responsiveness to her son and husband's angry outbursts as well as the roots her responsiveness had into her own developmental history. After 14 total sessions with this family Wayne's behavior at school and home was normal for a 16-year-old adolescent. Yes, he rolled his eyes and grumbled when his parents asked him to do something but his grades had improved from D's and F's to B's and C's with an occasional A. He was no longer a behavior problem at school or home. Dad was scheduling himself to spend more time at home because he had learned not be continually angry and disruptive. The family actually looked forward to dad coming home for a few days so that they could spend time with him, rather than dreading it and inventing ways to avoid him.

Parent's Role in the ADHD System

Parents are very much part of the ADHD system, both its cause and its cure. Parents of ADHD children have a higher incidence of anxiety (Biderman, et. al., 1991), major affective disorders (Biderman, et. al. 1991, 2), and coercive interactions (Danforth, et. al. 1991). Both parents of ADHD children tend to be more depressed, and such families have a higher divorce and separation rate (Brown & Pacini, 1987; Brown et. Al., 1988; Brown & Pacini, 1989; Fergusson & Lynskey, 1993).

The level of the mother's depression is predictive of both family functioning and a child's behavior. Alcohol consumption is also higher in these families (Cunningham, Benness & Siegel (1988). Though raising an ADHD child is stressful on the family, this stress would hardly seem to account for this range of problems.

Not only is ADHD an adaptive response to the negative aspects of the child's environment, but the environment also must then adapt to the child's frustrating and disruptive behavior. ADHD research literature has documented that these children provoke negative and controlling interaction patterns from their families. This interaction becomes part of a positive feedback loop between the child and his family, which typically causes a severe behavior amplifier.

If one side of the positive feedback loop is changed, the other side (the child) also changes. For example, when the child is treated with stimulant medication, the family interaction pattern improves without other treatment (Barkley 1989b, Barkley and Cunningham, 1979; Barkley, Karlsson, Pollard, & Murphy, 1985). This clearly underlines the feedback loop nature of the problem.

One could think of this change in pattern being the result of the family's feedback loops being broken by the ADHD child, who is now responding less emotionally and with greater willful attention as a result of medication. In other words, he is providing fewer triggers to continue the repetition of the behavior amplifier.

Developmentally, one could reasonably expect that the parent's problems usually predate the child's. In my clinical experience, most of these problems long antedate the birth of the ADHD child, usually dating back to the parents' own childhood learning histories.

The parents' families were most often compromised by divorce, poverty, emotional, and drug/alcohol problems. The inherent instability (hyper-reactivity) of these families makes them more vulnerable to being co-opted into the destructive positive feedback loops between parents and children. These feedback loops intensify both the child's ADHD and the family's problems.

Thus, the parent's emotional and behavioral distress is part of the ADHD syndrome, affecting its cause, maintenance, unhappiness, and cure.

Without treating the family, the ADHD symptoms eliminated from the child by CAER can quickly be relearned and return. For example, if you extinguish the symptoms of an ADHD child but do not change the behavior of, let's say, a very critical father, the child will again begin to attentionally avoid in reaction to the barrage of criticism. No treatment provides a guarantee against further insult.

Implications of Parent Treatment

Most parents I talk with are highly motivated to help their child. They also intellectually understand most of what they need to do. They have read parenting books, ADHD books, consulted with their minister, their friends, and teachers.

The intent of their parenting is not to drive their child crazy because the parents are stupid or can't think of any other way to spend their time. Still, this is how many traditional treatment procedures approach these beleaguered folks.

Their predicament is like that of a dieter. In spite of their reading of diet books, their ordering of diet videotapes, diet audio tapes, TV exercise equipment, in spite of their enrollment in weight management programs, in spite of their "understandings," they still eat the brownie or, in this case, get sucked into some uproar with their child.

They do it not because they don't know any better. They do it because they can't stop that feeling of wanting to eat. The same thing happens with parents of ADHD children. The parents' behaviors are driven by their feelings. Therefore, more knowledge is seldom the key to better parenting, particularly at the beginning of treatment.

Yet, because parenting practices are feelings-driven, parents will resort to strategies that alleviate their feelings of anger, fear, anxiety, and guilt, feelings they experience during the problem situation.

For example, if the parents were raised in a family that fought, they may resolve never to repeat that mistake. So, when they sense a fight, they avoid the conflict. Or, if their dad was always angry and yelling, then, when they feel frustration, they get angry and yell. Or, if they were the older sister who had to take care of everyone else, now, out of guilt, they repeat the pattern.

Or, if they were the mediator between parents when they fought, today, conflict makes them anxious and they act as the peacekeeper. Or, if they were molested ... and so on and so on it goes.   There is an endless list of possibilities, all of them driven by underlying feelings that serve to distort parenting practices away from what most parents intelligently know to be the best approach. And since parents usually have a cognitive understanding of good parenting, more instruction in contingency management or the use of "time out" results in little gain.

Changing these feelings-based parenting practices requires more than training in parenting skills.   The underlying emotional patterns have to be eliminated so that parents can utilize their knowledge. Typically, this means parents must spend time in CAER therapy in order to extinguish their emotional triggers.

By dealing with the parent's own dysfunctional learning history, we break through the emotional barriers to using the knowledge they already have. Once that is accomplished with CAER, a little coaching to refine their parenting knowledge can be useful.

Coaching before extinction of emotional barriers is often pointless.   Parents just end up learning more strategies they cannot access because they are emotionally aroused.

Extinguishing Emotionally Provocative Cues

If one asks family members (or teachers) who are in negative feedback loops to describe a particular incident, descriptions will usually follow a pattern: "She said.... He said.... She said... etc."

The specifics will change from situation to situation, but the emotional language, tone, and structure of the description will stay the same. It is like a play that gets acted out over and over. Though the actors, scenery, and costumes change, the play goes on its destructive way.

However, it is not really the words that are the culprit; it is the emotions these words evoke in the person hearing them that drive the sequence. Their emotional responses to each other's words provide alternating links in a chain that manacles them together in destructive interactions. If these same words no longer elicit an emotional response, then the chain reaction dies, i.e. the next participant is no longer emotionally motivated to provide the next link in the chain.

To extinguish the emotional response from these loaded words, participants are asked to record their own brief audio tapes with the very statements that they make that provoke undesirable feelings and behaviors in others – the previously discussed tapes the parents make for their children.

This is just one-half of the story. The reactions of adults to the child are the other half. To augment this process, the child is asked to record on a five-minute audio cassette all the things he says that irritate his parents. These tapes typically include such statements as:

> "All my friends are....
> "I hate you..."
> "You can't make me..."
> "I don't have to..."

Parents, while on CAER, listen to the irritating tape. Their reaction is similar to that of their child. At first, these words are very upsetting. After listening to the tape a while, their response to these phrases decreases and then vanishes.

When the same words are then heard in real world situations, they continue to lack emotionally provocative power. This improves the parents' feelings toward their child and reduces emotional and behavioral reactivity to the child's misbehaviors.

Because of the lack of emotional arousal to these trigger words, the adult is better able to respond systematically and rationally. Using CAER to extinguish the parent's negative emotional responses to the child dramatically speeds the treatment process.

Extinguishing Parents' Personal Triggers

Parents also bring their own emotional baggage to their marriage and to parenting. Sometimes these emotional barriers keep parents from cooperating as parents. At other times, it distorts their responses to the child.

For example, a child might say, "I hate you" to a parent whose own parents said similar things to them. This may fire the parent's emotions so that instead of remaining calm and appropriately reactive to the child, he becomes enraged and screams back. Alternately, he may feel so destroyed that he will cease to make demands on the child out of fear that the child will not "like" him.

These both obvious and subtle dysfunctional emotional patterns are transmitted to the child and must be eliminated.

On CAER, sometimes the child's tape, when played for the parent, will similarly trigger emotions that are connected to historical memories. This can be used to follow the parent's current emotional conflicts, whether related to the child or not, back across the web of their own emotional learning history.

For instance, on CAER, the parent might start out thinking about how the child makes the mother feel so helpless. Once these helpless feelings are accessed, they then serve as a thread to follow back across the parent's life.

Following the thread is almost automatic. It might string to the husband and how he makes her feel helpless, the time when she felt helpless in a crowd, the eleventh grade science class where she felt helpless to understand, when her big brother held her down when she was nine, etc.

Though each of these elements has very different content, they share the same feeling, helplessness. Extinguishing this emotional thread eliminates its power to color interactions with her ADHD child and her husband. Behavior that formerly caused a feeling of helplessness no longer elicits helpless feelings in the mother. She is better able to do what she knows she "should" as a parent but has been unable to do because of the helpless feelings that were previously elicited. Then, what the child says or does no longer sets off the parent's negative emotions.

A Better Functioning Family System

It is also often useful to have parents record emotionally provocative tapes for one another. Then, just as they have done with their child, they listen to the other parent's tape while on CAER. This eliminates the emotional barriers that keep parents from cooperating to provide a unified parental voice in dealing with their children. It also usually improves the marriage.

The power of this two-way extinction of emotionally loaded words to reduce real world family and classroom chaos is usually very effective and sometimes astounding. In many ways, words are reality. The ability of these children to provoke others verbally makes their behavior seem much worse than it actually is.

They keep the adults around them so irritated with their words that there is very little tolerance for misdeeds. Once the verbal dimension is dampened, their behavior seems much more manageable. Everyone is more able to deal with problems rationally and intentionally.

For the child's part, compliance with adult requests is usually much better and less emotional. Excessive emotion does not keep the content of the message from being heard and responded to. This does not solve all of the family problems, but it usually has a dramatic impact on the angry encounters, which cause families to spiral downward very quickly.

Chapter 27

The Utility of Boredom Tolerance

Dealing with Boredom

Boredom, in the adult sense, is such a problem for children that it is worth exploring. For many people, and particularly children, the avoidance of boredom is a major motivator. Most parents are all too familiar with their child's "I'm bored" laments. For children, this avoidance of boredom, or it's inverse, looking for some excitement, can negatively reinforce problem behaviors that provide escape from the aversion of boredom.

Our culture presents two opposite perspectives about boredom. Children grow up in a high stimulus, multimedia world where everything pleasurable is labeled "exciting" — the exciting new this, get in on the excitement of that. Children from an early age expect pervasive excitement from their every waking moment. For them, that's the norm.

By contrast the behaviors, at least for school children, adolescents, and adults, which lead to success are not a multimedia experience. Beginning in elementary school and rapidly progressing though middle school, high school, college, and the work world, there is a strong demand to tolerate boredom.

As those of us who have earned college and post-graduate degrees can attest, the ability to tolerate and persevere through immense and sustained boredom is one of the major skills required for success in this culture. Our multimedia world does nothing to give us the mental skills to cope with the boredom required to achieve culturally defined success. If anything, it does the opposite.

One of the useful outcomes of CAER with ADHD children is to develop boredom tolerance. We tend to think of boredom as some type of void, emptiness, or blankness. Really, the experience of boredom for these children is a learned emotional response, which feels like a tense aversiveness or agitation. As such, it follows the same rules as any other learned behavior and can be extinguished by CAER.

When ADHD children first begin to follow their feelings of boredom on CAER, anger, fear, embarrassment, and frustration usually emerge. Over time, these negative emotions disappear, and the child begins to report feelings more characteristic of the adult experience of boredom.

If they continue to focus on this vaguely uncomfortable, tense feeling, it too will extinguish. All that is left is a relaxed, comfortable void. Extinguishing the boredom makes them more task-oriented and tolerant of the drudgery that they must realistically endure. It is no longer something to fight, but rather something that just must be done in the most efficient, least distressing way that can be invented.

Children tend to find this adult-like boredom the only aversive part of CAER therapy. When they begin to complain, we begin the process of extinguishing their stimulus expectancy to below what they are accustomed to in a multimedia world. The procedure lowers their stimulus expectancy for fast-paced entertainment in all settings.

By persevering on this path for a little while, these children become more tolerant of the true (adult sense) boredom that the culture demands of them for academic and vocational success.

Sometimes the boredom can be utilized in a therapeutic way. It provides receptiveness to establishing new behavior patterns by substituting Ericksonian style metaphoric stories for the music they listen to while on CAER. This seems to reduce boredom, while at the same time providing them with metaphoric models for their behavior. On the other hand, it seems unwise to eliminate totally the experience of boredom because one of the very useful skills that CAER teaches is boredom tolerance.

When nine-year-old Scott began to complain of boredom while on CAER, he was played a story about Chucko the clown. Chucko was a clown who did not practice his tricks and disrupted other circus performers when they practiced. Eventually he was taken out of the act because of how he acted. That made him very sad. He then worked hard and did not bother others when they practiced. Eventually the other performers allowed him to rejoin them in the circus performance. This story was a metaphor for Scott's classroom behavior. His mother said that he talked about the story all the way home. Whenever he would get off task his mother or teacher would gently ask him if he knew a clown called Chucko. This would remind him of the story and many times he would stop disturbing others and get back on task.

Boring classrooms are a reality that is unlikely to change. To survive in the classroom all the way through higher education, children need to learn boredom tolerance. Despite the boredom, children agree that CAER helps them. Many times, they are quite proud of their improved behavior and grades.

Chapter 28

Shaping New Behavior

A Case for Sudden Change

Dr. Greenspoon, an experimental psychologist, was interested in how the patient and therapist interacted in "Client-Centered Psychotherapy," which was popularized in the Fifties (Greenspoon, 1955).

He arranged a series of experiments in which an experimenter (graduate student) and a subject would sit and talk. Unbeknownst to the subject, the experimenter was systematically responding every time some small aspect of the subject's speech — such as plural nouns or the use of adjectives — was used. He responded by nodding or saying "uh ha," just as therapists do.

What Greenspoon found was that the subject's speech behavior quickly changed to produce more of the element that was being reinforced by experimenter responses. And the subjects were seldom aware of how the experimenter was controlling their speech.

Similar experiments have been successfully re-peated hundreds of times shaping just about every behavior you can imagine.

How Change Can Be Sabotaged

Similar shaping of behavior patterns happens in families and schools. Families often give a double message. They may say they want to change, but they operate as if they wish to stay the same. If you examine this at the individual level, the message is that each family member wants others to change to fit their behavior. "I'm okay, you're not." That's because change is hard work, so hard that it is always better for someone else to do the changing.

This pressure to undermine the change process is both explicit and implicit. It is as if the family requires the child to fit into a specific role in order for the other family members to know how to deal with him and for the family system to stay in balance. If the child does not play his role, the adults feel anger or rejection, even fear and frustration, over the elimination of his previous role.

As a consequence of this discomfort, the adults perform their half of the loop more intensely. This is in an attempt to get the child to return to his old dysfunctional role so that the norm returns and their own uncomfortable feelings will cease.

An example of this is when parents have a history of requesting that the child perform some positive behavior, like doing homework. The historical pattern is for the parents and child to have an escalating emotional exchange, possibly marked by yelling and door slamming, and little homework gets done.

After treating the child on CAER, the process is initially different. When the parent requests that the child does his homework, without protesting much, the child goes to his desk and begins work. An argument does not develop because the emotional responses to the parent's request for doing homework have been extinguished in the child.

However, though the situation has probably improved, it is still not what it should be or what the parent expects. Since the parent's strategy for getting compliance with homework is unchanged, the old pattern slowly reappears. As the child makes slow progress on the homework, the parent becomes frustrated and begins to become louder and more negative with the child. This begins to annoy the child and he reciprocates in kind. The emotional exchange is soon back to where it was before treatment.

Most times the process is much subtler.

The Greenspoon experiments help us understand another way family members are able to shape each other's behavior, including after one member changes his behavior and the family shapes him back into old patterns.

The historical pattern in a family might be that one has to get really loud and upset before anyone listens to his requests. Everyone has learned that they can tell what is important and what they need to respond to by the volume and emotion of the speaker.

The child is identified as the problem in this family and brought for treatment. After CAER, he is milder mannered and less provoked into this emotional fervor, but no one listens to his calm requests. When he is a little louder and more emotional, he tends to get more of what he wants. The family requirement to speak loud to be heard soon shapes his speech back to its prior loud emotional level.

In this way, the incongruent member (the treated ADHD child) of the family-school-peer social network can be re-shaped by the rest of the network back to where he was originally. This serves to fill the gap created in the system by his "cure." It happened once and, unless specifically prevented, it will happen again, since it is the easiest way for the system to come back into balance.

This is not an intentional, purposeful, or aware process but is built into the nature of social networks. Recidivism results from not adjusting the system as a whole. While the ADHD child is the targeted patient, the true identified patient is the system as a whole.

To deal with these types of problems, we must swiftly treat the whole family at once.

This bold strategy pays off well. This means that each family member needs to work on his own component of the family feedback loops. This eliminates a wide range of family patterns at the same time.

When they emerge from CAER, there is a void in the interaction patterns of the family. Each family member is attempting to reorganize their own internal system to a new homeostatic level, rather than trying to enforce the old interaction patterns. Thus, they have to invent new ways of interacting with one another because the old ways no longer have the emotional energy to drive them. Without the emotional baggage, families reorganize into healthier patterns.

Following CAER, they demonstrate that they knew all along how to interact properly, but it had been masked by historical emotional patterns.

Why? ... The Distinction between Cause and Maintenance

Many parents I talk to want to know why their child is ADHD. "Why" is an awfully small word to be as important as it is and mean as many things as it does. By "why," do we mean what started it, or do we mean what makes it happen today, or do we mean what can we do about it, or ...? Though why may have more meanings, these are the ones we need to discuss before we proceed.

We must distinguish between forces that begin a process from those that maintain it. Many processes could not get started without the initiating cause, but this first cause does not have the power to maintain the process once it is started.

Once started, a process must work in the environment or it will die for lack of reinforcement. Let us take temper tantrums as an example. A parent in a store refuses to buy a child a toy. The child then has a temper tantrum and lies on the floor screaming and kicking. The parents are very embarrassed, so they are tempted to give him the toy to get him to be quiet.

However, if the parent gives the toy after the tantrum, then the tantrum works to get toys, so it is more likely to be repeated. On the other hand, if the parent refuses to give in and just walks off leaving the child lying on the floor kicking and screaming, then the tantrum does not work. The probability of another tantrum is reduced.

Any number of random reasons such as having missed his nap, being cranky from being ill, or seeing another child have a tantrum may have caused the initial temper tantrum. It does not have to be intentional, and it does not make any difference why the first occurrence happened. It just happened.

The important aspect is whether this variation in behavior finds some utility in the environment. This utility has nothing to do with what caused the first tantrum. All that matters is whether the parent buys the toy. If it works, planned or not, the first step in a chronic behavior problem has been taken. If it does not work, no toy is bought. The variation in behavior is meaningless and is unlikely to reoccur.

As previously discussed, attentional avoidance of aversive stimuli begins the ADHD process. It continues to grow and generalize to other settings, subjects, and people, not because of the original incident of attentional avoidance, but because the strategy continues to work by increasing the child's pleasure or reducing his pain.

Chapter 29

Contingency Management: The U-shaped Curve

The Reinforcement Desert

The next step in our discussion is to explore how the world differentially reinforces good and bad behavior. Though CAER is useful to extinguish emotional learning history, one cannot ignore current reinforcement contingencies that shape the child's behavior. Current contingencies are tomorrow's learning history.

How the culture shapes behavior is not as straightforward as we might assume. There are forces that make individual change difficult for the child and those around him. One can visualize the distribution of reinforcers as a U-shaped curve. This curve describes the rewards that the child gets from a specific level of good or bad behavior.

Going either away on line *a-b-c* from the center of the curve increases the environment's response and thereby reinforcement to the child. The bottom of the **U** describes a deep, dangerous reinforcement desert that the child has to travel across. Traveling across this desert will take him from his antisocial ADHD behavior on the left cusp to positive, socially approved behavior on the right cusp.

An ADHD child on the left, anti-social cusp of the curve gets attention for irritating others. If the child wants more attention, the easiest way to get it is to move even further to the left on the curve by being even more irritating. He will then get more attention, yelling, hollering, etc.

His other option of moving right on the curve, would in the short term, be self-defeating. He would have to do less negative behavior, i.e. more positive behavior, for less reward — no attention. That makes no sense, though we regularly and blithely ask ADHD children to do just that and resent them for not complying.

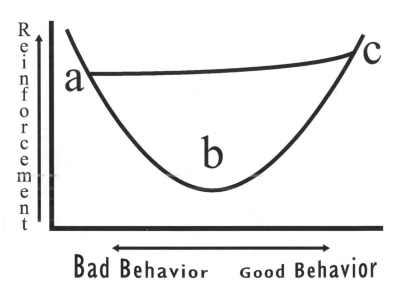

The horizontal axis describes the good - bad dimension of the child's behavior. The center is neutral. Going left from the neutral low point is toward bad, and right is toward good behavior. Good or bad is defined by the child's particular culture and how it responds to the child. The vertical axis represents the reinforcing response that the child gets from the situation for a certain level of good or bad behavior.

In other words, why would an ADHD child make efforts to improve his behavior if it initially results in a net loss of rewards.

Let us assume that the child is at point *a* on the left, "bad" behavior side of the curve. If he becomes more obnoxious (moves left on the curve), he will get more reinforcement such as parental attention for his misbehavior.

But we want him to move right toward better behavior (moving down from *a* to *b*). This means that he is going to decrease reinforcement all the way to point *b* before the payoffs start improving again, which may be quite awhile.

From the child's perception, there is not a smooth, even shift from a negative to a more positive behavior pattern. If he is on the positive (right) side, his most efficient way to get more reward is to be even more positive. If he is on the negative (left) side, then his most efficient way to get more reward is to become more antisocial.

This latter effect is very important. Being on the negative end of this curve is a trap that is hard to get out of without help or great determination. Once a child gets very far from the center of the curve, powerful forces push him out further and further. There is a major obstacle to getting the child re-engaged with the socially prescribed reward system of attending, compliance, and achievement. This is not a description of a conscious, willful choice by the child, but rather a description of how his environment responds to him.

Why the Reinforcement Curve is U-shaped

There are three reasons why this reinforcement curve is **U** - shaped.

(1) It is very difficult for parents to interact with their child without being reinforcing. Many parents try to punish their children by scolding them, pointing out their errors,

berating them, or getting mad at them. This seldom works for more than a moment because despite the attempt to punish, the parent is also giving the child full, undivided attention.

By virtue of the fact that the attention is coming from the parent, this is usually reinforcing to the child. Therefore, the child's behavior that precipitates the parent's verbal punishment usually increases in frequency. That is, it is reinforced.

Sure, children find positive interactions like praise, hugging, food, and privileges more rewarding than verbal put downs, rejection, and grounding. But if the children cannot get the former, they will work for the latter. This may not be warm, loving, approving attention, but it still effectively reinforces the child's antisocial behavior.

(2) The reliability of the pleasant and unpleasant reinforcers is also quite different. The child soon learns that if he provokes the parent, he gets their reinforcing attention almost every time he acts out. However, for most parents the reinforcement schedule is leaner and more inconsistent for positive performance. Indeed, the child typically must do several positive things before an adult will respond.

The upshot is that the negative side has a much tighter linkage. With adequate intensity, a child can reliably get immediate parental attention for each disruptive display.

Therefore, the reinforcing effect of parents' attempts to punish the child, as well as the greater reliability of the child's ability to trigger this reinforcement raises the cusps of the **U**.

(3) It can also be very difficult to get parents and teachers to respond to more positive behavior by the child if more positive really means less negative.

If the child is not tearing the house apart, parents feel a sense of relief. Rather than rewarding the child with something positive for the reduction in chaos, they breathe a sigh, enjoy the peace, and quietly avoid the child in order not to provoke him into his normal disruptive behavior.

The child is descending (on Line **a-b**) into the reinforcement desert. At this point, if he acts in a more pro-social way, he will actually reduce his reward, and this will decrease the probability of more good behavior in the future. Each incident is "either part of the solution or part of the problem."

The child learns that there is more reinforcement for being a problem than for being better, even if the reinforcement is nothing more than being yelled at by an adult. As said before, being yelled at is better than being quietly avoided. This mechanism deepens the bottom of the **U**.

Parents and teachers sometimes have a hard time understanding that it is not how they meant something, but how it was understood and experienced by the child that makes the difference. They repeatedly say, "We try to...," "I meant that ...." It is the result, not the intention that defines the meaning of the statement. If the resultant behavior increases, then it empirically is reinforcer, no matter how it was meant.

Left of center on the curve is where the ADHD child operates. CAER can release him from the learned, emotionally driven responses, that trigger the ADHD child's dysfunctional behavior. However, if these behavioral changes are not captured by the pro-social reinforcement from the right side of the curve, they have a tendency to be re-trained right back.

So how do we solve this problem?

Daniel – A 9-Year-Old Behavior Problem

Daniel was a very skilled nine-year-old ADHD family disrupter. Before his parents came to see me, they had unsuccessfully tried many behavior therapy techniques to improve his behavior. They had offered him rewards at the end of the week if he was better that week. They grounded him when he misbehaved. Though he would resolve to work for these rewards, he was seldom successful. In fact, he spend much of his time grounded from his favorite activities.

In discussing these problems, his mother exclaimed that he drove her nuts. She was constantly yelling at him, to which he paid no mind. She had read several parenting books and knew that she should not do this. But she could not help herself when he would tease his sister, sass back at her, yell and make other noises or refuse to do his homework. She was out of control, and had recently started taking tranquilizers to help calm her down.

I explained to her what was happening in terms of the **U**-shaped curve. There were opposing forces controlling Daniel's behavior. Daniel was someplace around *a* on the curve. He could move to the left by getting his mother yelling. He was doing to her what he likes to do with the family dog.

He would play with the dog by taking him out in the back yard and wrestle, chase and tease the dog until he was barking and jumping around. This was fun for both Daniel and the dog. It was equally fun to get his mother to yell as it was to get the dog to bark. He could get this reward, of getting his mother to yell, very quickly.

His other choice would be to move down the curve *a* to *b* by irritating his mother less. His mother would likely be relieved but would be unlikely to provide much reward.

To get much reward for better behavior, he would have to traverse the *b-c* part of the curve by doing positive acts like his homework. The problem is that Daniel would have to wait a long time to get much payoff.

Therefore, the quick and easy way to get some fun was to annoy his mother to the point that she would start yelling, just like the dog would start barking.

In looking at this situation, I explained that there were two things we could do to help Daniel. We could make the reward of her yelling less available to Daniel, and we could make sure that he got some rewards sooner than point **c** on the curve. But, we had to create the **a-c** curve. Creating that **a-c** curve would be rough in the beginning. We had to make sure Daniel's reward system provided short-term payoffs, probably on a daily basis. This would produce a bridge over the reinforcement desert.

She could see the truth in my analogy, and she assured me that now that she understood, she could solve the problem without further assistance. She resolved not to fall into Daniel's trap anymore. As I expected she was not able to follow through on her resolve. She continued to yell at him.

To solve this, we did two CAER sessions on Daniel yelling at her. During CAER therapy, I first had her relive her experience of Daniel taunting her and she yelling at him. I then had her follow that same feeling back across her life. This led back to experiences of her father and mother fighting and yelling at one another. This made her feel frightened and helpless.

Daniel's yelling and fighting brought up those same unresolved feelings. That made it much harder for her to respond rationally to his acting out. Once these feelings were extinguished, she was able to utilize her knowledge of good parenting, stop reinforcing Daniel's negative behavior, and start reinforcing the positive.

Daniel's behavior improved quickly and dramatically.

Building the Reinforcement Bridge

We solve the problem, first, with intervention. The intervention must start where the child is, not where we want him to be.

Therefore, the contingency managers in his world — such as parents and teachers — have to be sensitive and responsive to the baby steps the child makes toward the positive behavior, even though the desired behaviors may not yet be at the level the contingency managers want. And, they have to be alert and responsive so that they systematically support not just pro-social behavior, but behavior that might simply be less anti-social behavior.

They do this by artificially building a line from *a* to *c* across the curve. This *a-c* line will then serve as a bridge from antisocial antics to pro-social behavior. In fact, as illustrated by line *a-c*, this bridge will be a continuous path of gently increasing rewards for the child — a bit like dropping a trail of Gummy Bears for him to follow to a prize for everyone. Such rewards will slowly move him from the "bad" (left) side of the curve to the "good" (right) side of the curve.

The bridge also avoids the impossibility of trying to force the child to travel through the reinforcement desert at the bottom *b* of the curve.

This reinforcement re-engineering has to take place at two levels. The first is the obvious — contingency management. The second is only slightly less obvious — extinguishing the adults' negative learning history.

As stated previously, contingency management, or applying rewards for less negative behavior, does not work for long because the parents' emotions drive their actions as much as the child's emotions drive his behaviors. And so, if the parents' underlying emotions are not dealt with, the parents' actions will eventually force the child back into his old negative behaviors.

This can be seen in how parents' breathe a sigh of relief and quietly avoid the child when the chaos stops, not because they think that this will teach Daniel to behave better, but for their own emotional relief.

This lack of responsiveness to the child's improved behavior rests on the parents' emotional history of annoyance by the child. It is this manifestation of the **U**-shaped curve resulting from the parents' emotional conditioning, not their logical, cognitive, intentional actions, that makes a difference.

Thus, for the child's reinforcement curve to follow the slowly rising *a-c* line, this annoyance that creates the **U**-shaped curve must first be extinguished. And that brings us to the second level — treating parents (and ideally teachers!) with CAER to extinguish their emotional responses that lock them into the dysfunctional pattern.

Once the emotional foundation for the dysfunctional **U** pattern is extinguished, the parent's cognitive knowledge and convictions can then guide their behavior until a new emotional foundation can be built. This foundation will be built out of a more positive interaction with the child, not on annoyance, but on pleasure and approval.

Let me emphasize one more time, contingency management systems, such as contingency contracts, point systems, or other structured reward systems, can be powerful temporary aids to get the child plugged into the positive side of the curve. The key word here is temporary.

The idea is to build a bridge, not a fat cat lifestyle for the child. Ultimately, the child's positive behaviors have to be maintained by the reinforcers that naturally occur on the positive side of the **U** curve.

Why Ritalin Alone Doesn't Work Long-term

ADHD is not an infection that is killed and is over with. It is an interaction pattern with the child's environment. The learning history can be controlled with Ritalin or extinguished with CAER, but if this window of opportunity is not seized upon by creating the *a-c* line, the same environment will shape the same behavior again.

Most ADHD children who come see me are on Ritalin or other stimulant drugs. The parents say they know the drugs help because when they forget to give their child his pill or attempt to take him off it, he gets worse. Therefore, the pill helps, or at least it used to. They are not sure. When they first put him on the drug, he got better, they say, but over time his behavior worsened, almost to the point of where it was before.

This is exactly what one would expect if the environment is re-shaping ADHD after it was controlled with Ritalin. The sudden change in the beginning is the Ritalin providing the child with the willful attention to control the negative behavior. The degeneration of his behavior over time is the retraining of the ADHD behavior by the environment.

When he is taken off the Ritalin, parents face the anti-social behavior that Ritalin originally helped control as well as the more recently learned "bad" behaviors that have been created since starting medication. In other words, parents then face a double whammy to have to deal with.

In a sense, the Ritalin has helped the child dig himself into an even deeper hole. In my experience, these children are more difficult to help than those who have never been medicated.

Windows of Opportunity

The parent's relief from the child's prior aversive behavior usually results in reduced vigilance on their part, as the **U** - shaped curve predicts. Instead, there should be an intensive effort to capitalize on the temporary improvement, i.e. on this window of opportunity.

In fact, creating a window of opportunity is pointless if it is not utilized. And if it is not utilized, the window will close with little changed, except sometimes for the worse, by one more disappointment. Indeed, most windows are missed because they are misunderstood to be a fix of the "deficit," rather than a temporary pattern change and an opportunity for permanent change.

This is abundantly clear with the small window opened by the administration of stimulant drugs. Even though there is clear consensus that stimulants should be combined with behavior therapy, as noted earlier (Newsweek, March 18, 1996), most children with ADHD who are prescribed stimulants are not referred for behavioral treatment.

CAER can create a strong, long lasting window of opportunity by improving the child's attentional participation in his immediate world. However, no technology can provide a permanent cure if the child's situation is not changed at the same time. So, if this positive engagement is not rewarded, further attentional avoidance is likely to be relearned, just as the original was learned.

In other words, emotional patterns that drive the **U** - shaped curve must be extinguished. And that must be done before willful efforts to prop up the *a-c* curve can be successful. CAER treatment with the whole family generates a window of opportunity for change for each family member. Stimulant medication only provides the child with a window of opportunity that is small and unstable.

Missing the Window of Opportunity

Physicians miss this critical window of opportunity because they understand themselves to be treating a stable neurological defect in the child, not a dynamically changing, learned attentional pattern that must be unlearned. Most often the narrow window of opportunity created by Ritalin is not utilized because the timing issues are not understood.

Stimulants are commonly given by the family physician or pediatrician before or without referring the family to a psychologist skilled in dealing with these children. Only after the drug fails, i.e., the window of opportunity is closed, is the family referred to a psychologist.

If stimulants are to be used, though I prefer CAER, then therapy with the child and family needs to be concurrent with the INITIAL trials of stimulants. The family and school need to be prepared to take advantage of the narrow window. By doing so, we increase the chance that the environment will reinforce these new efforts by the child and that his efforts can then succeed.

Chapter 30

Discipline

Abdication of Parenthood

Another parenting problem, which is on the increase, is a trend toward abdication of parenthood. More parents are looking to professionals, schools, and medications to manage their child, rather then asserting their parental role. Many parents are emotionally intimidated by their own children.

When I suggest to these parents that they punish their child, they retort, "That will make him mad." And I respond, "Then you know you are being heard." My lack of concern or even applauding their child's unhappiness is bewildering to some parents. They see their job as pleasing their children rather than training him to be a good person, student, and citizen.

On an abstract level, they believe this, but on a moment to moment basis, they are not willing to face their child's emotional wrath. The child's assessment of the desirability of their actions becomes the meaningful index, rather than adult parental wisdom. Abdication is the easy way out. The family has become child-driven rather than adult led.

When I suggest to parents that their child should do his homework after school, before play, the parent will turn to the child and say, "Listen to what the doctor tells you." They are making it my problem to get the child to do his homework. In other words, the parents are trying to make me the parent.

These same parents are eager to put their child on Ritalin or blame the school for their child's problems. They are parents who have their own issues with self-confidence, self worth, and assertion.

Though I try to push their parenting responsibilities back on them, it usually does little more than momentary good. Usually only when their own personal issues are resolved can adults begin to assert their parental demands on their children. If being a parent does not feel good or elicits anxiety, they are not going to do it for long. Their own self worth, self confidence and self-esteem issues must be dealt with before they can be assertive parents. CAER extinguishes the emotional obstacles to being the good parent that most parents wish to be.

Grounding Children

Some of the most convenient strategies for reducing undesirable behavior are techniques such as time out, taking privileges away, making the child go to his room, grounding, and so forth. These approaches work, not because they are really aversive, but because they interrupt the child's flow of reinforcement. Since there are many long and detailed treatises on these behavior therapy techniques, I will only cover them briefly.

When I suggest such approaches to parents, they often tell me they have tried them and they do not work. Upon further examination, though, it is apparent why they fail. Timing and intensity are key if such approaches are to work. Since the goal is interruption of reinforcement, it is essential that the time out or removing of privileges be applied as quickly after the offending behavior as possible — much like the hangover coming upon first drink, rather than the morning after, as discussed earlier.

If the child who causes a disruption at the dinner table is not sent to his room immediately, his disruption is likely to be reinforced by further arguing, playing with food, or the other children laughing. If he is not sent to his room until after dinner, the effects will be greatly weakened because the short-term reinforcers at the table are more powerful than the longer term punishment. So swift justice is essential.

The other issue is intensity of the time out from reinforcement experience because it is important that reinforcement drop very sharply. To explain, many parents tell me they have grounded their child for months at a time. On the surface this sounds horrendously cruel. Usually when we discuss what grounding really means, the grounding is far from severe enough to be effective.

By grounding many parents mean something to the effect that the child cannot spend time with his friends after school, but he can still use the TV, phone, computer, and toys. On weekends he can go to the mall or to sports practices. Grounding turns out to be only a minor annoyance to the child.

A much more effective approach is to ground the child severely for a short time. Grounding might be cleaning everything but bare essentials out of the child's room, making him go to his room immediately after school, depriving him of the use of the phone, TV, computers, friends, or toys. He stays there except to go to the bathroom and school. Dinner is brought to him.

Though the experience is intense, it only lasts for one to three days. Such short, intense strategies work much better and are more humane. Sometimes more than time out from reinforcement is required.

The Liability Issues of Corporal Punishment

To say anything about the use of punishment, particularly corporal punishment, other than disavowing it, exposes one to serious liability risks. In reading this chapter on punishment, you are agreeing to take full and total responsibility for determining the suitability, veracity, and utility of the concepts and procedure described below.

It is highly recommended that you consult with your advisors, such as your physician, attorney, mother-in-law, clergy, child protective services, God, and any one else who wants to carry the liability issues with you, before you make any decisions about these ideas.

In sum, what you do with these concepts is totally your responsibility, not mine. Got it?

If you do not agree to these terms, do not read the rest of this chapter on punishment.

ICBM of Discipline

Well, I guess you have decided to read on, but remember it is all yours to decide.

Since punishment is so ubiquitous, no discussion of behavior management would be complete without a discussion of corporal punishment. Punishment is used excessively and ineffectively in this and most cultures. Many problems we have with the legal system, the penal system, ADHD, and psychophysical disorders can be traced to the inappropriate use of punishment. I am not an advocate of the widespread use of punishment, but like a spice, a little bit well-placed can add a lot. So, here goes.

I hate to be walking through Safeway watching a mother swat her child on the rear every time he touches something. Most of these kids do not even look around when they get hit, they just get a little longer stride from the energy of the impact. The swat does not hurt that much, so it has been easy for them to learn to ignore it. They have developed attentional avoidance for the sting on their rear just as they later learn to avoid the emotional sting of math class. The parent's low-level pecking away with the swat is analogous to the low-level pecking that the math teacher does verbally. Both are easily adapted to with attentional avoidance. Both make ADHD worse.

This brings us to rule one: NO pecking.

Either make the punishment severe enough that it breaks through the attentional avoidance and makes a significant impression, or don't punish at all.

This, in turn, brings us to the ICBM (Inter Continental Ballistic Missile) principle. Remember the days of the Cold War with the Russians, when John Kennedy would sit eye-to-eye with Nikita Kruschev, each with their back pocket brisling with ICBMs?

None of these ICBMs was ever fired at one another, nor were they ever intended for that purpose. They were something to point at as a threat. John Kennedy's message was, in effect, "If we can't negotiate this my way, then I will shoot my ICBM at you." (Luckily, we had bigger and better ones and they knew it.)

Punishment, particularly spankings, should be used the same way. Probably not more than three or four spankings should be necessary in a childhood, but they need to be ICBMs. I am not advocating child abuse. I am advocating creating something you can point at later as a marker.

It is not just the pain of the hand across the bottom that makes a spanking work, it is the whole experience. Some old-time parents knew about this. They would tell their child that he would be getting a spanking later. The child would have to sweat it out for a couple of hours. When the appointed time would arrive, the child would have to go cut his own willow switch and pull his pants down.

The parent would stomp, scream, and rage, while giving him a few solid whacks. The spanking is not just the whack, but the whole dramatic, psychological performance calculated to make an ICBM quality impression. Later this ICBM can be pointed to just as JFK did. When things get out of hand, the parent can firmly say to the child, while looking him straight in the eye, "Are we getting ready for a spanking again." If you have built a true ICBM, you have the child's complete attention and he is wanting to know what it is that you require.

The time for the next spanking is not dictated by the level of your next fit of anger with the child, but when, "Are we getting ready for a spanking again?" does not bring the child's complete attention.

Is this child abuse? That is for you to decide. Our aversion to punishment is one of the reasons we have had to turn to medications for behavioral control of our children. Even for those who see the merits of a good spanking, be they parents or teachers, the social and legal risks of being accused of being a child abuser are high.

Because of this, we elect to abuse our children in more socially prescribed ways such as drugs, school failure and continual nagging. I think that three or four meaningful spankings per child are much less abusive and more useful in producing good behavior. Constantly swatting a kid just teaches him better attentional avoidance, so you can give him Ritalin later.

As I said before, punishment in any form has to be used like a spice, very little placed precisely in the context of the other elements of the meal. Punishment has to be one small part of a basically positive, reinforcing parenting program.

Punishment overall is not very effective and creates many problems of its own; so do not rely on it too much.

Briefly, punishment fails on two counts. It elicits negative emotions toward the punisher, and it does not generalize to other situations.

For example, most of us drive too fast when no cop is in sight. When a police car comes on the freeway, we are good little citizens and go exactly the speed limit. When the punisher, the cop, pulls off the freeway, we speed up. If the cop does catch us and writes us a ticket, we are mad at him. Most of us do not like cops very well because of these experiences.

It is the same with children trained via punishment. When dad is home everything is in order. As soon as he leaves, things go to hell. If dad metes out much punishment, then the children dread dad's coming home.

Like a spice, punishment if done well is very useful, but overdone the whole meal is ruined.

Chapter 31

Paving the Way for Rational Problem Solving Approaches

CAER and Rational Thought

Emotions have a way of preempting rational problem-solving. When the emotional reactions are eliminated, there is time for a person to think and evaluate the pros and cons of other possible actions. Since after CAER treatment more behavior is guided by rational willful functions, as opposed to emotional automatic processes, more benefit can be gained from techniques that refine rational functions, i.e. rational thinking.

With CAER treatment, the balance between these two functions shifts so that logical control of behavior becomes more prevalent and relevant. Once the emotional reactions are extinguished, there is time and ability for the child to think and evaluate the merits and consequences of alternate actions.

He then acts more in terms of his long-term best interests, rather than on his impulses and emotions. Since this type of process is the root of rational persuasion, logical control of behavior returns. The child is then accessible to persuasive control of his behavior by others.

As these conditioned emotional responses are extinguished, compliance improves markedly. Instructions no longer seem aversive to the child and can be evaluated intellectually, without the conditioned emotional response. They are responded to in a more socially appropriate manner. When the parent says, "Clean up your room," the child has no conditioned emotional response.

He rationally evaluates the request something like this:

"Well, if I don't clean up my pig pen, I may be grounded. If I do clean it up, they'll let me go to Jason's after school. I could clean it up now, but I'd have to give up the TV program I'm watching. If I do it later, I won't have time to go to Jason's. I think it'd be better to clean it up now."

And he says, to Mom's utter astonishment, "All right." And he goes and does it. She thinks he is trying to please her. He is not. He is simply acting out of his calculated, rational sense of personal self-interest, rather than presenting a conditioned emotional response.

Learning Access

Some children who have suffered from ADHD for a long time have very large academic skill deficits that are difficult for them to make up. To assist this catch-up process I have developed an academic tutoring program I call Learning Access. Unlike traditional tutoring, Learning Access is not more of the same. It is uses CAER to extinguish the emotional roadblocks to learning during the tutoring process, so that acquisition of skills happens more rapidly.

How Learning Access Tutoring Works

In traditional tutoring, the same negative forces that caused the initial deterioration of performance continue to degrade the student's performance. This is because he continues to experience aversive feelings with educational tasks. Traditional tutoring often fails because it just presents another opportunity for the child to rehearse his emotional blocks to learning.

To be successful, tutoring must resolve these emotional blocks, while also teaching content, rather than simply providing another opportunity to experience aversive feelings while trying to learn. The Learning Access program focuses on resolving the blocks to learning in tandem with teaching the subject content.

Resolving Blocks to Learning

As discussed throughout the book, many learning problems are a result of emotional responses to the learning situation rather than some inherent defect in the child's neurology. The child becomes so angry, anxious or depressed that he cannot pay attention and learn effectively.

These feelings are often set off by specific cues in the learning situation, such as the learning materials themselves. Changing these emotional responses typically resolves the resistance to learning and promotes learning in a much shorter time than is possible when the tutor is fighting the child's distraction from the task.

The Learning Access program uses CAER to extinguish the emotional barriers to learning rather than just continuing to rehearse them. It extinguishes the anxiety, anger, frustration and other negative feelings as the tutoring takes place. When the tutor detects an emotional block to the learning, the child is switched to

CAER for a few minutes to eliminate the negative affect interfering with the learning.

In fact, learning practice and CAER are alternated to first elicit the emotional blockage then to extinguish it with CAER. Using this procedure, we have helped children in a few sessions to achieve substantial academic gains. Often, their parents had spent a great deal more time and money in more traditional tutoring programs without success.

Who is Learning Access For?

Learning Access is useful for children with learning problems who are not showing signs of more pervasive emotional problems, such as anxiety, depression, ADHD or severe behavior problems. Because it is important to make sure more pervasive emotional issues are not present, a brief evaluation is performed on every child to determine if they can immediately enroll in Learning Access or whether psychological treatment is first necessary to resolve broader emotional issues.

Chapter 32

A Final Note

Within the Solution was the Solution

My own voyage through ADHD has lead to the development of a new conception of ADHD and an innovative treatment for this problem that plagues millions of children. These ideas would not have been possible without my own many hours over six years in the CAER machine. I was only half of a creative loop that resulted form my iterative interaction with CAER. This self-therapy provided me with the mental and emotional state that allowed me to create its next evolutionary improvement, which in turn enhanced its ability to carry me further. Though it certainly never added one word or idea to this book, if it were not silly to have an illiterate machine as a co-author, I would certainly have credited it.

But, thank you Mr. CAER for helping me slay Mr. ADHD.

Epilogue

Treatment Resources and Web Page

Since Spokane, Washington, is currently the only place where CAER treatment is available, we are able to accommodate families by offering very short-term, intensive Treatment options. This allows a family to use an intense, week-long visit to make swift changes in their ADHD-plagued family.

I hope this book will generate the funds and interest that will allow me to establish more convenient locations across the nation. Until then, we are working to be as flexible and innovative as possible in developing services to help those far from Spokane. You can discuss the options with us by calling my office (509) 448-6462. My E-mail address is **weathers@caer.com**, and my web site **http://www.caer.com**.

Other Applications of CAER

ADHD is only one of the many areas that can be treated with CAER. We have successfully treated a wide range of physical disorders that are induced or exacerbated by stress. The following is a very brief summary of some of the problems that have been helped by CAER treatment. A more in-depth explanation of the treatment of these disorders is in progress.

Childhood Sexual Abuse

CAER has been used in the treatment of female and male survivors of childhood sexual abuse. Adults who have been abused as children often experience anxiety disorders, depression, shame, poor self esteem, difficulty in relationships, as well as flashbacks and intrusive memories of the abuse.

CAER has helped these victims work through the many negative feelings they experience as a result of the abuse. Treatment involves focusing on the unpleasant feelings and images until they are desensitized. Negative perceptions of oneself often change dramatically within a few sessions.

Marriage Problems

Therapy with couples focuses on two goals. The first goal is to extinguish the negative emotional history that partners bring to a relationship and that interferes with their healthy functioning as a couple. The second is extinction of the negative interaction patterns that have developed in the relationship.

A standard procedure has evolved over the dozens of couples I have treated. In the first session, I assess their interaction pattern and problems, while developing rapport with them. For the most part, in subsequent session, I treat them individually.

CAER is used to accomplish the first goal of extinction of negative emotional history. The patient traces back across his or her life the negative feelings connected to relationships. This process is repeated until the current negative feelings, as well as those on the affective chain dating back to the original experiences, are extinguished.

The second goal, extinction of negative interaction patterns that have developed in the relationship, is addressed by presenting each of the spouses with the verbal interpersonal cues that trigger conflict.

Each of them takes home a five-minute cassette and records both sides of the tape with all of the things they say that demean, provoke, and irritate the other partner. When they return for their individual session on CAER, they listen to their partner's tape, which is designed to provoke negative feelings in them.

Listening to these emotionally loaded words on CAER desensitizes them to these statements so that the next time they occur in the relationship, a conditioned negative emotional response does not preclude humor or problem solving.

Once the current emotional cues and the historical links to them have been extinguished for each spouse individually, their interaction usually improves markedly. Usually in less than six sessions each, the marriage problems are solved and they are communicating well, with no training in communications.

Our follow-up is casual and not as thorough or comprehensive as we wish, but it is apparent that this procedure works better and more quickly than the numerous other techniques we have tried over the years. My book on the treatment of couples will soon be published.

Panic Disorder

We have successfully treated more than 25 cases of panic disorder using CAER. The majority have been successfully treated in two to five sessions; others have taken somewhat longer. Patients are first asked to re-experience a recent panic attack, then trace that panic feeling back through each panic attack they have had, all the way back to the first attack.

They stay with each recalled panic experience until the emotional arousal abates completely; then they move to the next experience. Although other competent practitioners had treated several of the patients for some time without success, after just one-hour of CAER patients experienced relief of the majority of their symptoms.

Successive sessions were only necessary to deal with long- term learning history issues that could have caused the problem to reoccur. Follow-up over a two-year period has indicated that there has been little relapse.

Asthma and Respiratory Allergies

We have successfully treated more than 30 cases of asthma. The asthma cases treated so far seem to be a form of panic disorder that focuses on the respiratory system. As with panic disorder, treatment involves having the patient remember the experience of prior asthma attacks. This always causes a minor asthma attack while on CAER. The patient stays with the asthma attack experience until it abates, usually in less than 10 minutes. These patients all carry inhalant medication, but never has anyone had to use it during CAER treatment.

The experience of the asthma attack is used as an axis for an affect bridge to previous asthma attack experiences. Each of these remembered asthma attacks causes a successively smaller asthma attack. This procedure is continued until memories of asthma attacks elicit no emotional or physical response.

Asthma patients who have exercise-related asthma are asked to either bounce on a trampoline or run stairs until they precipitate asthma symptoms. They then do CAER until the symptoms abate. This process is repeated until they can no longer trigger asthma symptoms through exercise. Usually only three or four cycles are necessary.

Many asthma patients also have respiratory allergies, such as to animal dander, grasses, flowers, and pollen. CAER treatment of asthma includes the extinction of these allergic responses. Patients take a small baggy of each allergen into the CAER machine with them. Once they are in the relaxed CAER state, they open one baggy and inhale it until they get strong allergy symptoms like restricted breathing, plugged sinuses, and runny eyes. They then close the baggy and focus on the allergy sensations until they abate, which is usually five to twenty minutes.

Once the symptoms abate, they open the same baggy and inhale as before until the symptoms are stimulated again. They then close the baggy and again focus on the symptoms. This cycle is repeated until it no longer produces any symptoms.

The whole process is repeated with each baggy they take into the CAER machine until none of them will cause any symptoms. Real world symptoms usually disappear after one session as described above. As a preventative measure, an abbreviated version is usually repeated the following week.

Follow-up after four years shows no relapses.

As an added note, the most common treatment for asthma is an inhaler. Though the risk of dying from asthma is small, the use of an inhaler doubles the risk (Winslow, 1991). CAER offers a risk-free treatment alternative.

Irritable Bowel Syndrome (IBS)

For many patients, the onset of Irritable Bowel Syndrome (IBS) can be traced to an emotionally laden event or illness. The use of CAER to extinguish these underlying emotional precipitants of IBS tends to relieve symptoms. 64 patients have been treated for chronic irritable bowel syndrome. Using CAER they have been markedly improved, such that they no longer require medication to remain symptom free. My book, *IBS: A Path to Success* will be available mid 1998.

Depression

Depression is the most common and complex pathology that has been treated with CAER. The treatment of more than 400 depressed patients usually has involved having the patient focus on the current experience of depression. By means of an affect bridge, the patient traces this experience back across this learning history. The patient is usually able to go back to one or more early experiences that first initiated the depressive affect.

The affect is extinguished from these early memories by repeatedly recalling and re-experiencing them. This process is typically repeated many times until all of the affect is extinguished from the toxic memories that can be recalled. Mood often improves after the first session. Five to 10 sessions are typically required in the majority of cases to resolve the depression.

Appendix

Speculation on Possible Neurological Mechanisms for CAER and EMD/R

At this point, no one knows the neurological mechanisms that are responsible for the effects produced by CAER or EMD/R. There are some clues about possible mechanisms, but be assured that at this point they are just speculations.

Let me offer you my preferred explanation, if for no other reason than for your intellectual stimulation.

Similarity to REM Sleep & Lucid Dreams

Dreaming is one of the natural ways we process upsetting events in our lives. If I wreck my car today, I am likely to dream about it tonight. Dreaming about my wrecked car helps me resolve some of my feelings about being in an accident so that I feel better. This is one way we naturally process many things that disturb us.

When we dream, our eyes move rapidly back and forth, which is referred to as Rapid Eye Movement (REM) sleep. In REM sleep the rapid eye movement is caused by a part of the brain called the pons (McCarley, Winkelman, & Duffy, 1983). With CAER, the rapid eye movement of sleep is simulated by following the moving lights and sound. Whether caused by a part of the brain or by moving lights and sounds, a similar mental state is elicited. Thoughts, images, and feelings experienced while on CAER, like those experienced in dreams, over time lose their ability to cause emotional arousal.

It is theorized that REM sleep is the closest natural mental state to that produced by CAER. Studies of REM sleep deprivation clearly demonstrate the necessity of REM stage sleep. If subjects are allowed to sleep all they wish, but are awakened whenever they go into REM sleep, in a few days they become floridly psychotic. They will experience severe hallucinations and confusion. These symptoms quickly go away when they are again allowed REM sleep. REM sleep is critical to sanity.

Lucid dreams are a light form of REM sleep in which we are aware that our dream experience is in fact a dream. Sometimes you can willfully guide a lucid dream. The CAER experience is like one of these willfully guided lucid dreams only a bit more conscious.

Reciprocal Inhibition of Visual Attention and Eye Movement

From clinical experience it is apparent that CAER effects are the result of a disinhibitory process. The puzzle is how moving lights and sounds should cause these phenomena. One clue is provided by Fischer & Breitmeyer (1987), who propose a mutually inhibitory relationship between eye movements and visual attention.

This implies that visual attention must be disengaged for there to be eye movements. Since CAER orchestrates continual eye movements, it follows that this process would maintain a continual inhibition of visual attention. The critical point is that without visual attention processes psychological defenses systems cannot be accessed. This exposes traumatic memories, which we normally scrupulously defend, to the natural process of extinction.

Defenses serve both a good and bad function. On the good side, they keep us from experiencing current and past emotional trauma. Attention is just shunted away from the stimuli so that our experience is diluted or blocked. This makes our experience of the moment more pleasant.

If something terrible has happened to us, such as being abused as a child, we have the memories of those occurrences stored in our minds. These memories carry with them many of the awful feelings of the original experience. If these memories were to pass continuously through our consciousness, we would experience these bad feelings frequently. In order not to feel bad all the time, our defenses work hard to keep those traumatic memories out of consciousness. When we sleep, our defenses may come down enough for these memories to surface, and they are experienced as nightmares.

The negative side of defenses is that traumatic memories remain so closely guarded from our experience that we prevent the bad feelings from being extinguished. Extinction does not happen without emotional experience. Since the traumatic memories are diligently defended, there is no alternative but to keep storing them up one after the other. Over time more and more energy must go into the defense process to keep these memories out of consciousness. Thus less energy is available for productive activities. Extinction of these emotions releases the energy typically used by the defenses. This leads many people to feel euphoric for a few days after a CAER session.

A mid-brain structure, known as the superior colliculus, may be involved in calling up defenses (Dean, Mayhew, & Langdon 1994). It controls both eye movement and visual attention. CAER "ties up" the eye movement part of this structure directly and indirectly occupies visual attention processes. The superior colliculus' capacity is then occupied making it more difficult to call up specific defense systems. The emotionally loaded memories are now forced to the surface.

Because they are no longer inhibited by defenses, they are free to come to the surface, i.e., consciousness. When the emotions linked to loaded memories are extinguished, they lose the power to intrude into consciousness. They are then experienced as boring rather than upsetting. This is clinically known as desensitization.

Neither CAER nor EMD/R are Hypnosis

One of the common misunderstandings about CAER is that "it is just like hypnosis."

Not so.

Though hypnosis and CAER have a deep relaxation component in common, they are very different phenomena. In hypnosis the patient is usually mentally lethargic, and the therapist takes major responsibility for directing the process. The therapist is talking much of the time (i.e. hypnotherapy), directing the patient to feel this, imagine that, or do the other.

In CAER the patient is much more alert and directs the therapeutic process himself. The therapist only occasionally intervenes to guide the therapeutic focus. In many ways CAER, as I said at the beginning, is do-it-yourself therapy. The CAER machine sets up a therapeutic state. The therapist provides starting points and occasional consultation. The patient, the world's expert on himself, directs the therapy on a moment to moment basis.

From the patient's point of view, it feels like a passive rather than a self-directed process. It is experienced as a dream or movie unfolding rather than "Let's see, what is the next thing I should think about?"

Because of its ability to follow emotional themes, the subconscious mind directs itself to the emotionally loaded events that are then brought to consciousness and extinguished. Extinction happens because the feeling is triggered in an artificial situation that does not provide a reinforcing consequence. Our nervous system is configured so that behaviors without consequences are extinguished. And emotions are a form of behavior.

Bibliography

Abikoff, Howard. (1991). Cognitive training in ADHD children: Less to it than meets the eye. *Journal of Learning Disabilities,* 24(4), 205-209.

Ambady, N., & Rosenthal, R. (1992) Thin slices of expressive behavior as predictors of interpersonal consequences: A meta-analysis. *Psychological Bulletin, 111,* 256-274.

Barkley, R. A. (1990). *Attention deficit hyperactivity disorder.* New York: The Guilford Press.

Barkley, R. A. (1989b), Hyperactive girls and boys: Stimulant drug effects on mother-child interactions. Journal of Child Psychology and Psychiatry, 30, 379-390.

Barkley, R. A., & Cunningham, C. E. (1979). The effects of methylphenidate on mother-child interactions of hyperactive children. Archives of General Psychiatry, 36, 201-208.

Barkley, R. A., Karlsson, J., Pollard, S., & Murphy, J. (1985). Developmental changes in the mother-child interactions of hyperactive children. Journal of Abnormal Child Psychology, 13, 631-638.

Bandura, A. (1962). Social learning through imitation. In M. R. Jones (Editor), *Nebraska symposium on motivation:* 1962. Lincoln: Univ. of Nebraska, 211-269.

Biderman, Joseph; Baldessarini, Ross J., Wright, Virginia; Knee, Debra et al. (1990). A double-blind placbo controlled study of desipramine in treatment of ADD:I. Efficacy. *Annual Progress in Child Psychiatry & Child Development,* 481-497.

Bohline, David S. (1985) Intellectual and affective characteristics of attention deficit disorder children. *Journal of Learning Disabilities.* 18(10), 604-608.

Borden, Kathi A.; Brown, Ronald T.; Jenkins, Philip & Clingerman, Stephen R. (1987). Achievement attributions and depressive symptoms in attention deficit-disordered and normal children. *Journal of School Psychology,* 25(4), 399-404.

Brown, Ronald T.; Borden, Kathi A.; Clingerman, Stephen, R. & Jenkins. Philip. (1988). Depression in attention deficit-disordered and normal children and their parents. *Child Psychiatry & Human Development,* 18(3), 119-132.

Brown, Ronald T. & Pacini, Joseph N. (1989). Perceived family functioning, marital status and depression in parents of boys with attention deficit disorder. *Journal of Learning Disabilities,* 22(9), 581- 587.

Carlson, Caryn L. & Brunner, Melissa R. (1993). Effects of methylphenidate on The academic performance of children with attention-deficit hyperactivity disorder and learning disabilities. *School Psychology Review,* 22(2), 184-198.

Chew, P.H., Phoon, W. H., & Mae-Lim. H.A. (1976). Epidemic hysteria among factory workers in Singapore. *Singapore Medical Journal 17,* 10-15.

Chelune, G.J., (1986). Frontal lobe disinhibition in attention deficit disorder. *Child Psychiatry and Human Development 16,* 221-234.

Cummings, E. M. (1987). Coping with background anger in childhood. *Child Development, 58,* 976-984.

Cunningham, Charles E.; Benness, Barry B. & Siegel, Linda S. (1988). Family functioning, time allocation and parental depression in the families of normal and ADHD children. *Journal of Clinical Child Psychology,* 17(2), 169-177.

Cunningham, C. E., Siegel, L. S. & Offord, D. R. (1985); A developmental dose response analysis of the effects of methylpenidate on the peer interactions during treatment. Journal of Child Psychology and Psychiatry, 26, 955-971.

Danforth, Jeffery S.; Barkely, Russel A. & Stokes, Trevor F. (1991). Observations of parent-child interactions with hyperactive children: Research and clinical implications. *Clinical Psychology Review,* 11(6), 703-727.

Davis, m. R. (1985). Perceptual land affective reverberation components. Lin A. B., Goldstein & G. . Michaels (Eds.), *Empathy: Development, training, and consequences* (pp. 62-108). Hillsdale, NJ. Erlbaum.

Dean, P., Mayhew, J. W., & Langdon, P. (1994). Learning and maintaining saccadic accuracy – a model of brain-stem-cerebellar Interactions. *Journal of Cognitive Neuroscience, v. 6,* p. 117-138.

Downey, G., & Coyne, J. C. (1990). Children of depressed parents: An integrative review. *Psychological Bulletin 108,* 50-75.

Ebrahim, G. J. (1968). Mass hysteria in school children: Notes on three outbreaks in East Africa. *Clinical Pediatrics, 7* 437-438.

Fein, (1981). Pretend play in childhood, and integrative view. *Child Development, 52,* 1095-1118.

Fischer, B. & Breitmeyer, B., (1987) Mechanisms of visual attention revealed by saccadic eye movements. *Neuropsychologia, 25,* 73-83.

Fisher, S., & Fisher, R. L. (1993) *The psychological adaptation of absurdity.* New Jersey, Lawrence Erlbaum Assn.

Gammon,G Davis & Brown, Thomas E. (1993). Fluoxetine and methylphenidate in combination for treatment of attention deficit disorder and comorbid depressive disorder. *Journal of Child & Adolescent Psychopharmacology*, 3(1), 1-110.

Goleman, D. (1989, March 28). The root of empathy are traced to infancy. *New York Times*, pp. B1, B10

Greenspoon, J. (1955). The reinforcing effect of two spoken sounds on the frequency of two responses, *American Journal of Psychology*, 68, 409-416

Grenell, M. M., Glass, C. R., & Katz, K. S. (1987); Hyperactive children and peer interaction: Knowledge and performance of social skills. Journal of Abnormal Child Psychology, 15, 1-13.

Hancock, Lynelle (March 18, 1996). Ritalin. *Newsweek*, 129, 64-70.

Headstrom, (1991). A note on eye movements and relaxation. *Journal of behavior Therapy and Experimental Psychiatry*, 22, 37-38.

Hatfield, E., Cacioppo, J.T. & Rapson, R. L. (1994). *Emotional Contagion*, Paris, France :Cambridge University Press.

Hatfield, E., & Sprecher, S. (1986). *Mirror, mirror: The importance of looks in everyday life.* Albany, NY : SUNNY Press.

Higgins, E. T., (1989). *Knowledge Accessibility and Activation: Subjectivity and Suffering from Unconscious Sources, In Unintended Thought*, James S Uleman & John A. Bargh, Eds., The Guliford Press, New York.

Hirschfield L.& Gelman, S. Eds; (1994), Mapping the mind, Domain Specificity in Cognition and Culture, Cambridge University Press.

Kaufman, A. S. (1979). *Intelligence testing with the WISC-R.* New York: John Wiley & Sons.

LaBerge, S. (1985). *Lucid dreaming.* New York: Ballantine Books.

Logan, G. D., & Cowan, W. B. (1984) On the ability to inhibit thought and action: A theory of an act of control. *Psychological Reviews, 91,* 295-327.

Marquis, J. N. (1991). A report of seventy-eight cases treated by eye movement desensitization. *Journal Behavior Therapy & Experimental Psychiatry, 22*(3), 187-192.

Marsh, E. J. & Johnston, C. (1982). A comparison of the mother-child interactions of younger and older hyperactive and normal children. Child Development, 53, 1371-1381.

Mattis, S., French, J.H., & Rapin, I. (1975). Dyslexia in children and young adults: Three independent neurological syndromes. *Developmental Medicine and Child Neurology, 17(2)* 150-183.

McCarley, R. W., Winkelman, J. W., & Duffy, F. H. (1983). Human cerebral potentials associated with REM sleep rapid eye movements: Links to POG waves and waking potentials. *Brain Research, 274,* 359-364.

Milich, Richard & Okazaki, Mimi. (1991). An examination of learned helplessness among attention-deficit hyperactivity disordered boys. *Journal of Abnormal Child Psychiatry,* 19(5), 607-623.

Mischel, W. *Personality and assessment.* New York: John Wiley, 1968;

Puk, G. (1991). Treating traumatic memories: A case report on the eye movement desensitization procedure. *Journal of Behavior Therapy & Experimental Psychiatry, 22(2),* 149-151.

Reay, M. (1960). "Mushroom madness" in the New Guiena Highlands. *Oceania, 31,* 135-139.

Resnick, L. B. (1994). *Situated Rationalism: Biological and social preparation for learning* in Mapping the mind, Domain Specificity in Cognition and Culture, Lawrence Hirschfield and Susan Gelman, Eds; Cambridge University Press.

Rosenthal, & Jacobsen, L., (1968). *Pygmalion in the classroom: teacher expectations and pupils development.* Troy, MO: Holt, Rinehart, and Winston.

Shapiro, F. (1989a). Efficacy of the eye movement desensitization procedure in the treatment of traumatic memories. *Journal of Traumatic Stress, 2*(2), 199-223.

Shapiro, F. (1989b). Eye movement desensitization: A new treatment for the post traumatic stress disorder. *Journal of Behavior Therapy and Experimental Psychiatry, 20,* 211-217.

Watkins, J. G. (1978). *The therapeutic self.* New York: Human Sciences Press.

Winslow, R (1991, Agust 9). Treatment of asthma could change. *Wall Street Journal* p. C11

Wolpe, J. (1973). *The practice of behavior therapy.* New York: Pergamon.

Wolpe, J., Abrams, J.(1991). Post-Traumatic stress disorder overcome by eye-movement desensitization: A case report. *Journal of Behavior Therapy & Experimental Psychiatry.* 3, 22(1) 39-43.

Zametkin, A. J., Nordahl, T. E., Gross, M., King, A.C., et al. (1990) Cerebral glucose metabolism in adults with hyperactivity of childhood onset. *New England Journal of Medicine, 3223 (20),* 1361-1366

Zbrodoff , N. J., & Logan, G. D. (1986) On the autonomy of mental processes: A case study of arithmetic. *Journal of experimental Psychology: General, 115,* 118-130.

Index

A

B

C

F

family therapy 164
fear 26, 47, 48, 54, 74, 79, 81, 113, 120, 123, 124, 130, 132, 211, 228, 249, 252, 256, 260
feedback 35, 44, 53, 74, 75, 79, 83, 136, 141, 161, 162, 183, 184, 193, 200, 210, 230, 248, 250, 262
fibromyalgia 127
Freud,Sigmond 50

G

Gestalt Therapy 128, 137
Goodman, Ellen 78
Greenspoon 306

H

homunculus 92, 93
hyperactivity 197, 199
  hyperactive 28, 202, 303, 304, 307
hypnosis 300

I

impulsive behavior 61, 173
inhibition 73, 116, 117, 123, 153, 162, 175, 176, 177, 179, 180, 234, 298, 299
intervention 86, 125, 240, 271
Irritable Bowel Syndrome 127, 296

J

Jensen,Peter 120

L

labels 27, 28, 53, 128, 197
  label 191
language 87
Learning Access 286, 287, 288
Learning Disabilities, LD 27, 127, 128, 177, 203, 204, 205, 209, 211, 212, 244, 303, 304
Learning Model 57, 148, 150, 152
Lupus 127

M

male
  boys 41, 81, 82, 83, 137
manic-depressive
  bipolar 201
marriage problems 292
mechanical model 148, 149, 150, 153, 154, 155, 157,
    158, 159, 162
medication 17, 62, 118, 139, 141, 142, 160, 192, 219,
    248, 274, 275, 294, 296
Methamphetamine 199

N

Neurochemistry 111
Nintendo 30, 34, 39, 59, 61, 70, 105, 106, 107, 108,
    118, 123, 205, 213

O

Occam's Razor 5

P

panic disorder 294
Paxil 199
Perls, Fritz 128
Piaget, Jean 157
Positron Emission Tomography
  PET 108
Prozac 130, 199
psychopathology 50
punishment 43, 65, 66, 70, 80, 105, 160, 161, 163,
    176, 199, 202, 268, 279, 280, 281, 282, 283, 284

R

Radk-Yarrow, Miron 167
Rapid Eye Movement
  REM 298
reinforcement curve 267, 272
reinforcers 105, 128, 129
  negative 30, 46, 178, 210, 265, 268, 273, 279
  reinforcement 42, 43, 44, 45, 199

About the Author

The author is an ADHD kid made good. He earned a Ph.D. in child clinical psychology from Peabody College of Vanderbilt University in 1974. He is a Diplomate of the American Board of Medical Psychotherapy. Before moving to Spokane in 1978, he was Director of the Adolescent Unit at Central state Psychiatric Hospital in Nashville TN, Director of the Family and Children's Achievement Center in Miami FL, Director of the Adolescent Unit at the Florida Mental Health Institute, and later Professor and Director of Research and Evaluation at the Florida Mental Health Institute at the University of South Florida in Tampa, Florida.

Though he has numerous professional publications, this is his first offering to the popular press. His background straddles psychology and engineering. In the late 60's he was a system's engineer for IBM. Later he founded a company to develop software to score and interpret major personality and intelligence tests (MMPI & WISC/WAIS). In the late 80's these software packages were sold worldwide.

His affection for technology goes back to his pre-teen days when he developed his first working fuel injection system that successfully ran on his father's pickup truck. As a teen, he put big engines in little cars (hot rods). After becoming a psychologist, he developed an electronic prompting device to speed psychotherapy and psychotherapeutic board games to structure inexpensive group therapy to treat large numbers of people inexpensively.

Since leaving the academic world, Dr. Weathers has worked in private practice with his psychologist wife, Mary. He has been working with children and families for more than 25 years. He and Mary chose Spokane because of their interests in back packing, hiking, mountaineering, telemark skiing, and bicycling.